I0038947

Quarterly Essay

CONTENTS

Quarterly Essay is published four times a year by Black Inc., an imprint of Schwartz Media Pty Ltd. Publisher: Morry Schwartz.

ISBN 978-1-86395-498-3 ISSN 1832-0953

Subscriptions – 1 year (4 issues): $49 within Australia incl. GST. Outside Australia $79.
2 years (8 issues): $95 within Australia incl. GST. Outside Australia $155.

Payment may be made by Mastercard or Visa, or by cheque made out to Schwartz Media. Payment includes postage and handling.

To subscribe, fill out and post the subscription card or form inside this issue, or subscribe online:

www.quarterlyessay.com
subscribe@blackincbooks.com
Phone: 61 3 9486 0288

Correspondence should be addressed to:

The Editor, Quarterly Essay
37–39 Langridge Street
Collingwood VIC 3066 Australia
Phone: 61 3 9486 0288 / Fax: 61 3 9486 0244
Email: quarterlyessay@blackincbooks.com

Editor: Chris Feik. Management: Sophy Williams, Caitlin Yates. Publicity: Elisabeth Young. Design: Guy Mirabella. Assistant Editor/Production Coordinator: Adam Shaw. Typesetting: Duncan Blachford

TRIVIAL PURSUIT

Leadership and the End of the Reform Era

George Megalogenis

Elections are a form of peer-group pressure, in which leaders are bullied into being as small-minded as the public at its worst. Yet voters are not so stupid that they can't see their knees being jerked. In 2010 Julia Gillard and Tony Abbott broke the democratic contract with a campaign so awful that it begged a collective rebuke.

I hadn't seen anything like it in more than twenty years of covering national affairs. It was a flip of a coin who was the more annoying: the robotic prime minister or the relentlessly negative Opposition leader. I wanted to pen a resignation letter to my employer: "Dear Rupert, sorry, I can't pretend that this contest is worth reporting. Neither candidate deserves to win. Julia won't talk the country up; Tony keeps talking it down."

Two amiable and intelligent politicians had frozen, together. They delivered no memorable quotes, let alone policies – merely slogans that quickly became punchlines at their own expense: "moving forward" and "the real Julia" versus "stop the boats" and "end the waste."

The quick, and romantic, conclusion to draw is that the people willingly smashed the machine by choosing none of the above on 21 August. To borrow one of Kevin Rudd's better mantras, Australia declared that this reckless style of campaigning must stop. That may be true, but I wouldn't take the next step and assume that a hung parliament is the solution to a crisis of governance that has been a decade in the making.

Today there is a whiff of the conflict-ridden 1970s in the air. The main parties have nothing to offer their supporters beyond conspiracy theories about their opponents. Labor blames the media and a bloody-minded Opposition for the shrill tone to the national conversation. The Coalition points the bone back at Labor, which it accuses of being the worst government in history.

Business and organised labour have assumed the right of veto over policies they don't like, and they spend millions in advertising to make their point. News organisations engage in turf wars, most notably the ABC and the *Australian*. The media reflect and reinforce the malaise through the restless search for another scandal to fill the 24-hour news cycle.

The election year felt like one long domestic dispute. The row didn't end with Rudd's dumping as prime minister; it just took another screwy form as Gillard and Abbott competed for the right to shrink the nation. In no previous post-war campaign had both sides agreed to reduce the immigration intake regardless of the economic cycle. Ben Chifley and Robert Menzies would turn in their graves if they knew their political grandchildren could be so easily intimidated by public opinion.

The extraordinary thing is that Australia has never looked more appealing to the rest of the world. Whenever a government minister attends an international forum, the first question they are asked is, "How did you guys do it?" By this the questioner means: how did we avoid the global recession?

The 2010 campaign was the sound of a nation needlessly fracturing. Each side of politics clung like a barnacle to its version of reality. It is rare for the main parties to talk themselves into opposite corners of a room. One or the other has usually had a strong enough sense of where the majority sits to lay claim to it. But Gillard and Abbott, and behind them their poll-obsessed teams, were so terrified of offending the disengaged that they forgot to inspire the voters who were paying attention.

The Australia that revealed itself at the ballot box on 21 August was split every which way. Between the mining states and the southern states. Between men and women. And between old and young. The criss-cross of moods sent two unmistakable messages. To the Liberal Party and its coalition partner, the Nationals – Australia still leans centre-left, even in the bush. To the Labor Party – you blew it.

Australians elect Labor governments to change things. They never give them large majorities, but they reward them with successive terms if they can look after the heart as well as the hip pocket.

The contract between voters and Coalition governments is less demanding. Conservatives invariably take office in a landslide and hold power for long stretches, provided that they don't inflict a recession on middle-income earners or unsettle them with a broken election promise such as WorkChoices.

These differing expectations make for a double standard that Labor people revel in because it fits with the heroic notion that theirs is the party of progress. But it also means Labor cannot afford to run a do-nothing government because Australians will mark it more harshly than the Coalition when it fails to deliver reform.

The issue that triggered Labor's loss of face in 2010 was climate change. Kevin Rudd had presented it as our greatest moral and economic challenge. So when he shelved his emissions trading scheme (ETS) in April, without so much as a sit-down press conference to explain why, his personal approval rating collapsed. He followed the backdown on climate change with a fight over the taxation of mining. Rudd wanted to prove he still had vision and strength, but he picked an issue that was too complex to be digested in the time he had left before the election was due to be called. The so-called resource super profits tax clarified why our system had lost its ability to solve problems. The government dropped the tax on the community with no warning in the week before the May budget. The Opposition didn't pause to digest the merits of the tax because it saw a political opportunity in obstruction. The miners went to war with an advertising campaign that tested the limits of our democracy. The media, transfixed by the prospect that Rudd might lose his job, surrounded the combatants like the crowd at a schoolyard brawl, willing each side to keep punching.

Labor let Tony Abbott get into its head. The Coalition's campaigns against the emissions trading scheme and the mining tax assumed that households were one electricity bill away from bankruptcy. Party polling showed that Abbott had a point, but not the one Labor latched onto. Concerns over the cost of living were most acute in Queensland, where Labor had the most marginal seats on the line. But Labor's majority wasn't under threat until it ran away from its own values. The mining tax wasn't a significant vote-switcher in the end, but climate change was, because Julia Gillard finished on the same hesitant page as Rudd. Her poll ratings, and Labor's, began to slide again after she announced that she would consult a citizens' assembly before legislating to put a price on carbon pollution. Leadership and conviction were at issue once more.

Conservatives see the defeat of the ETS and the 2010 election result as important shifts in the national mood. They interpret the fall of the British Labour government and the mid-term elections in the United States as signs of an international swing back to the right. The ballot box tells a different story, because Australia still leans centre-left. The most relevant statistic is the combined primary vote of Labor and the Greens. On 21 August, it was 49.8 per cent, only 1.4 per cent below the record of 2007. The Coalition primary vote was 43.6 per cent.

Labor rises at the two extremes of our economic cycle: in wartime or recession, as it did with John Curtin's government in 1941 or Bob Hawke's in 1983; or at the top of a boom, as was the case with the doomed trio of James Scullin in 1929, Gough Whitlam in 1972 and Kevin Rudd in 2007.

At both ends of the spectrum, voters expect basically the same thing: more government intervention. In recession, they trust Labor over the Coalition to defend the social safety net. In boom time, they trust Labor over the Coalition to invest the proceeds of prosperity in social services and infrastructure. The twenty-first century has added climate change, water security and broadband to the traditional public-policy concerns of health, education and transport. This has reinforced the centre-left mood for the time being because these new challenges assume an active role for government.

As the lawyer said in *The Castle*, it is also about the vibe. Boom-time Australia is less greedy and less confrontational than it is in the acquisition phase that follows a recession. Even television programming has become warmer and fuzzier in recent years. Today viewers prefer the everybody-wins group hug of *MasterChef* or *Spicks and Specks* to the back-stabbing and grasping of *Big Brother* or *Who Wants To Be a Millionaire*.

The centre-left passed the right in the second half of 2005, according to Newspoll, as the WorkChoices legislation was being rushed through parliament and the China-led resources boom first began showering the budget with windfall revenues. Yet in retrospect the Ruddslide of 2007 was less significant than it seemed for Labor because even then it was being driven by the Greens. Labor won 52.7 per cent of the vote after preferences, but its primary vote was the lowest for an incoming government in the post-war era. At 43.4 per cent, it was around 6 per cent less than when it seized power in 1983 and 1972.

Plot Labor's primary vote over the past 100 years and two periods fall off the graph: the horror of the 1930s when the Scullin government was smashed after one term, and the decline since 1990. Between 1940 and 1987, Labor recorded just one primary vote below 40 per cent, in 1977. In the eight elections between 1990 and 2010, five have been in the 30-something death zone.

The party is a perverse victim of the Hawke–Keating economic miracle. The proportion of blue-collar workers has declined over the past twenty-five years. Professionals have taken their place, and they are drifting to the Greens.

Labor has traditionally worried about its male right flank, because of the split with the Democratic Labor Party in the 1950s and '60s and the more recent assault from John Howard. To get the DLP voter back, Gough Whitlam had to break Labor's hard-left faction in Victoria. This didn't offend the party's base because it dragged Victoria closer to the centre-left, where the rest of Labor's constituency already was. To meet the Howard challenge, Labor tried to edge to the right on the issue of border protection. Fine in theory, because that's where the nation was in the early noughties. But it doesn't work so well in a centre-left phase because for every conservative voter Labor rescued from the clutches of the Coalition, it lost another on its left to the Greens. The added complication is the feminisation of the workforce, which has made Labor generally more popular with women than men. Ordinarily this would have broadened Labor's base through the acquisition of conservative working women. But Labor lost as many women to the Greens as it did men.

The 2010 election should have marked the formal confirmation of power for the centre-left, with Labor winning a second term in its own right and the Greens claiming the balance of power in the Senate. It took an idiosyncratic prime minister and an inexperienced government to turn its mandate to mud. No other first-term Labor government has done so little with so much goodwill behind it. Past Labor governments could be trusted to hit the ground reforming in their first term. John Curtin recast the federation at home by claiming the income-taxing powers from the states. Gough Whitlam opened the door to relations with China. Bob Hawke floated the dollar. Even the successors to Curtin and Hawke made history in their first terms. Ben Chifley introduced the post-war immigration program and started the Snowy Mountains Scheme. Paul Keating delivered universal superannuation.

It is impossible to imagine modern Australia without these reforms. So what happened to the party of progress such that its return to power in 2007 found it unready and unable to lead?

The Rudd enigma explains some of it. He came to office with more than 600 promises to implement and a determination to win every day in the media. Ambition and indecisiveness linked arms to create an unusual model of leadership. Rudd talked, and talked. In the end, he was all doorstop and no delivery.

But Rudd was also the symbol of an era in which politicians viewed the electorate through the wrong end of the telescope. He wanted to be judged by his numbers, so he sweated the small stuff of the 24-hour news cycle and the fortnightly Newspoll. He tried to deal with the fragmentation of post-tariff Australia with a persona for every demographic. There was Kevin the erudite for the ABC set. Kevin the dag for FM radio and the Twitterverse. Kevin the genial dad for the Seven Network's *Sunrise* program. Kevin the bloke for *Today Tonight* and *A Current Affair*.

This wasn't an exercise in leadership but a form of politics as celebrity. The dignity of the office of prime minister has been reduced in stages since the 1980s. Hawke was the first rock-star prime minister, Howard the first common man to use talkback radio. Rudd wanted to be Hawke and Howard, so no medium was too trivial and no question too small for him to answer. An excess of accessibility diminished him so that voters could no longer discern between a major statement and a stage-managed appearance.

The responsibility must rest with the Labor caucus for giving Rudd the idea that government was just about him. Labor was dangerously short of institutional memory after eleven years in opposition, and it was happy to defer to the outsider who had finally beaten Howard for them. Only two ministers had previous experience in government: Simon Crean and John Faulkner. Crean says the Rudd model for governing didn't suit Labor because it placed too much emphasis on central control. The big decisions were taken by the so-called gang of four, namely Rudd, Gillard, treasurer Wayne Swan and finance minister Lindsay Tanner. When the kitchen cabinet met, ministers would be joined by advisers and bureaucrats.

"Narrowness in terms of cabinet processes can never work, particularly for Labor governments," Crean says. A reform-minded government shouldn't be afraid of internal debate:

> The concept of a smaller group for hard strategic decisions, I don't disagree with. But you've got to get the right mix between making the final decision and the consultative process that leads you to it.

I think also there was a tendency to use and justify the strategic priorities and budget committee of cabinet [the gang of four] because of the threat of leaks, but my very strong view in all the cabinets I've sat through, seldom was there a leak out of cabinet. Now I'm not saying it didn't happen. But I think the more you understand the sanctity of the cabinet room and appreciate it for that, that's your best sanction against leaking, or idle tongues. And the great irony is the leak that almost rocked Kevin, the Godwin Grech leak, was [due to] the surplus of *bureaucrats* in the room. We were not operating as a cabinet, but a technocracy on many occasions.

Rudd inherited a command and control structure from Howard. In Howard's final year, the Department of Prime Minister and Cabinet "provided about 7500 detailed documents or briefings for the PM," Howard's former press secretary David Luff revealed. "Twenty a day. Every day. John Howard is to blame. Centralisation expanded under his watch. To cope with his hands-on approach, PM&C evolved to give competing, complementary advice, independent of others."

All that information, and still Howard lost office at the top of a boom, while Rudd couldn't hold it together for one term and his party lost its majority and almost surrendered government after it replaced him.

What is going on here? One explanation is that Rudd misread his majority, and with it the nation. Rudd was, essentially, a leader out of step with the public, a conservative with a centre-left majority. Rudd thought the nation was where he was, serious but cautious. But they wanted substance, and a little fun. Rudd didn't go to war for his side, as Keating, Hawke and Whitlam had before him. He hoarded political capital when the polls were strong, so that he had nothing to show his supporters, the people who brought him to office, when his approval rating collapsed.

Another explanation is that neither Howard nor Rudd could tame the media in the digital age. They confused presence with persuasion. They assumed that people were listening when the polls were in their favour. When a difficult issue arose, they tried to contain it by changing the topic.

A cynical, though understandable, judgment was made about the electorate's attention span. The less the people thought, the better for the incumbent. Or so the theory went. But this method of feigned dialogue denied government a genuine connection with the community. Compounding the error was the desire to "win" each day's media – that is, to dominate the reporting. By definition, Rudd and Howard couldn't reshape public opinion to promote reform because they weren't prepared to tolerate a strong opposing voice as part of the process.

But neither of these explanations is sufficient. We are dealing with a system-wide crisis. Labor was unable to fulfil its first-term promise to be an agent of change because it, and the nation it served, had already lost the institutional means of reform.

The ETS and the mining tax and the back-sliding on immigration reflect the policy cowardice of the times. I will use these case studies to show why the reform model is broken, and that the Hawke and Keating governments, and the Howard government until 2000, knew a better way to run the nation. Consider what follows a medical examination of an ailing body politic. Let's start with the stethoscope: the media.

Kevin Rudd never lacked substance as prime minister. His critics who called him a phoney, most notably Tony Abbott, mistook absence of policy achievement for absence of vision. Rudd had belief, and a prodigious capacity for soaking up a policy brief. What he lacked was the patience to stick with a debate long enough to assure public support for his position. The global financial crisis was the exception that proved the rule. It was the only challenge big enough to contain his intellect and draw out his greatest strength in a genuine crisis, the ability to ask one more question of his advisers.

Early in his term, I dubbed him our first federal premier. My piece ran on the day of the 2020 Summit in April 2008, when the prime minister was just about at the peak of his popularity. It was prompted by Rudd's disconcerting habit of dashing from issue to issue. I explained all this to him over a cup of tea in Melbourne four days after publication.

He didn't tick me off, although I had been warned that he was upset. But he did tick off a long list of things the government was working on. Without realising it, he confirmed the suspicion that he had taken on so many projects that he might end up getting nothing done.

Rudd feared that if a leader didn't feed the media, it would eat the leader. His colleagues confessed on coming to government that they felt as if they were in competition with Britney Spears. The assumption was that if government ministers didn't turn up, their Opposition counterparts would. The danger of saying no to the media even once was that they would not be asked back.

Like every leader I've watched closely, Rudd was a media junkie. John Howard says he would have been a journalist if he didn't practise law before entering politics in 1974. Paul Keating still keeps a clippings file of articles that interest or annoy, and is a regular newspaper columnist and letter writer. Bob Hawke and Mark Latham both tried their hand as

60 Minutes reporters after they had left parliament. Tony Abbott and Malcolm Turnbull started out writing for the *Bulletin*.

Where Rudd parted company with his Labor predecessors was in having a severe case of journo brain – the condition that resets an adult's attention span to that of a five-year-old. This is not meant as a personal criticism, but rather a comment on a style of politics where winning that day's media overwhelms the business of government.

As with his centralised approach to governing, Rudd's media strategy was an extension of the previous regime's practice. The PM's press office operated like a mini publishing house. There were three press secretaries to put out the line and soak up the questions, and a battery of typists to pump out the transcripts of Rudd's every appearance. The bureaucracy was asked on almost a daily basis to produce what Rudd's people called "announceables" – some new piece of information or, if they were lucky, policy, which the prime minister could take with him to impress his media inquisitors.

Howard had developed the idea of an announcement a day to keep Keating off his tail in 1996. Howard's then chief of staff, Grahame Morris, explained the theory on the eve of that election. Policies had been held back deliberately so that the Coalition would have something positive to run with during the campaign. What are you guys going to cover, he asked: Keating attacks Howard, or Howard's latest announcement?

As prime minister, Tony Blair had a simple way to measure the demands of the 24-hour news cycle. He needed three issues a day to get him through his final election campaign:

> When I fought the 1997 election, we took an issue a day. In 2005, we had to have one for the morning, another for the afternoon and by the evening the agenda had already moved on. You have to respond to stories also in real time. Frequently the problem is as much assembling the facts as giving them. Make a mistake and you quickly transfer from drama into crisis. In the 1960s the government

would sometimes, on a serious issue, have a cabinet lasting two days. It would be laughable to think you could do that now without the heavens falling in before lunch on the first day.

What worked in a campaign quickly becomes an organising principle for a new government. Rudd made not one but three announcements in the week leading up to the 2020 Summit. He appointed the first female governor-general, introduced a price-monitoring scheme for petrol, and proposed to extend childcare. The first was symbolic, the other two were ideas that had already been trialled at a state level.

Rudd appeared to be made for the digital age. He was an all-thumbs blazing tweeter-in-chief with 800,000-plus followers. So long as his approval rating remained at Christ-like levels, the strategy seemed to be paying off. Senior Coalition figures confessed they were exhausted by the effort required to keep up with Rudd. But nothing he said stuck, apart from the odd, off-key quote such as "fair shake of the sauce bottle" or "political shitstorm."

Still, one can't blame Rudd for immersing himself in new media. Leaders have always looked for ways to cut out the press gallery and go direct to the voter, because they don't trust journalists to report their message faithfully. The digital age allows government and Opposition to become media organisations in their own right. They can direct their supporters to their home page, send them text messages, and encourage those who want to serve the cause to spread the word across the blogosphere. They are easy to spot. My niche economics and politics blog, *Meganomics*, is routinely bombarded with emails that begin with a patronising phrase along the lines of "I am a great admirer of your work, but you have got this one wrong." On one occasion during the 2007 election, I rang a contact and asked if he was behind that day's spike in traffic. Yep, he laughed. He had sent out a note to campaign workers at 11 a.m. that morning telling them to "jam" my blog.

Yet political parties can never hope to dominate cyberspace because technology has lowered the barrier to entry for lobby groups, granting them the same access to voters. GetUp! niggles Labor, the climate-change sceptics annoy the Coalition. The latter used email to mount a successful challenge to Malcolm Turnbull's leadership of the Liberal Party in late 2009; the emails created the impression of a mass movement. But come election day, the Climate Sceptics party didn't even cross the legal limit of credibility. They garnered just 0.03 per cent at the ballot box, with fewer than 5000 primary votes across the nation, which was less than half the number achieved by the Socialist Equality Party. But almost 5000 messages in a politician's inbox can seem like a lot of angry constituents.

The institution of the media is almost impossible to manage today because it no longer respects politics. This is not an active choice on the part of journalists but a consequence of the information revolution. Each new-media entrant affects the way the old media go about their work. When the 6 p.m. television news bulletins knocked off afternoon news-papers in the 1980s, the morning newspapers became more colourful. When talkback asserted itself in the 1990s, print journalists began to type as if they were shouting, and TV current affairs went from topical to trashy. The internet has made print even more aggressive and self-conscious, while forcing TV news into the credibility shredder of continuous broadcasting.

Old media have lost their financial power because advertising can no longer pay for large newsrooms. The evil genius of the internet is its ability to spook editors into cutting staff, while expecting more from those who remain. The demand for another story, another column, another bulletin, another live cross, routinely pushes the journalist into the gibberish zone. Too much information to process, too much to produce on any given day. What chance a considered policy debate?

Don't misread this as a cry for a slower, more liquid work day, when a long lunch could be rationalised as contact work. The internet has improved journalism in many ways. The problem is the black hole that comes with it. More news can't fill it because there are fewer reporters on the case. So we make up the difference with commentary. There is no right or wrong mix between news, analysis and opinion, but a form of medium creep is underway that turns journalist into player.

An article in the morning paper will prompt a couple of radio stations to call for a chat. Then Sky, then perhaps the *7.30 Report* or *Lateline*. Add another hour on the *Insiders* couch on Sunday, and it is conceivable that commentators will find themselves reheating the one insight across half a dozen forums. It becomes a form of politicking. A reporter goes on a virtual tour, like an author flogging their book. It is mostly harmless, until you count the hours that instant punditry takes away from the day job – time that used to be spent nagging sources, listening to debates and reading documents.

In this, journalists and politicians have converged in an alarming way: both the late Howard and Rudd governments spent far too much of their time feeding the beast. The result is a government that disappears up its own media mentions. In Rudd's case the problem began with him, but it also reflected the era. The pressure to be everywhere removed the sense of occasion when the prime minister spoke. There was no grand narrative to connect the individual announcements, only bewildering changes of agenda that left voters confused. One moment he was blokeing it up on a construction site, the next he was hopping on a plane to play diplomat at the United Nations.

Rudd didn't really know what he wanted to do with power. But even if he had had a plan, he would have found the media an unwilling conduit. To get his message to stick, he had to repeat himself. Neither Rudd nor the journalists had the patience for this traditional form of leadership.

I've witnessed three distinct phases in the relationship between politicians and the press. The 1980s was the incumbent's decade, when a federal Labor government convinced the press gallery that the Opposition was the better story. Labor used media monitoring to highlight rhetorical variations between Opposition spokespeople, and to play up the leadership rivalry between Andrew Peacock and John Howard.

We self-corrected in the 1990s by going on a form of government deathwatch, waiting first for the Hawke, then the Keating and finally the Howard governments to fall. In each case, our place in the pecking order was clear. They governed, we reported.

The past decade has diminished the influence of both leader and reporter. No one media group is dominant because the market is fragmented, but the media as an institution is more powerful than it should be because the never-ending news cycle has imposed a level of distraction on government that hobbles its ability to raise issues with the electorate. There is no tolerance for a long argument anymore because the public has been taught that every new day carries the promise of a blizzard of unique content.

The greatest threat the digital era poses to good government is not all those words, but the numbers. The desire for instant analysis leads politicians and journalists to the false comfort of the polls. There is a collective loss of confidence at work here. No one is really sure what voters will say to a new idea, so government and media ask them first through focus groups. It is no way to run a national conversation. Reform, by definition, must be preceded by a sustained debate. Rudd, and Howard before him, found that any issue that took more than a week or two to explain wasn't worth pursuing because they felt they couldn't afford the battering in the polls that this would entail.

Polling has been a necessary evil in politics for decades. The first poll of Australian attitudes was published in the old Melbourne *Herald* in October 1941, and no party has ever had the will to honour its findings. It showed 59 per cent of people favoured equal pay for women, 33 per cent were against, and 8 per cent were undecided.

The first major-party leader to be paranoid about the polls, and the media organisation that published them, was Robert Menzies. His antagonist was the Herald and Weekly Times's managing director and chairman, Keith Murdoch. In August 1947, the *Herald* advised its readers that Menzies was a drag on the conservative vote. "If a federal election had been held in July, with someone other than Mr Menzies as leader of the Liberal Party, it is possible that a Liberal/Country Party Government would have been returned to power," the first paragraph of the article read.

Menzies and Murdoch engaged in an angry exchange of letters that make the modern rumble between Labor and News Limited resemble a contrived bout of WWF wrestling. In one letter, Menzies asked Murdoch: "Can you really believe that you can strike down the leader of a Party – when you do not suggest any alternate leader in the Parliamentary rank – and do no injury to the Party?"

Still smarting a year later, and not yet in government, Menzies wrote a prescient column for the *New York Times* in which he said that leaders were "anxious" about the effects of polling "on the practice of politics":

> If it serves to tell the politician of widely entertained errors which he must attack, well and good. But if it merely tells him to beware, because opinion is against him, many good ideas will, I fear, be abandoned.

The early polls also showed voters were wary of the non-English immigrants that were coming from Europe. My favourite was taken in 1951, the year after my father migrated to Australia. The Gallup poll asked voters "whether or not Australia should get immigrants" from a list of seven countries.

The Netherlands (80.6 per cent), Sweden (76.8 per cent) and France (59.4 per cent) recorded strong yes votes. So my News Limited colleague Andrew Bolt, the offspring of Dutch immigrants, was meant to be.

But not me. At the other end of the scale, we said no to people from Greece (only 42.7 per cent of Australians wanted them, which was lower than the yes vote for Malcolm Turnbull's republic). At least my mother country was close; Yugoslavia (33.5 per cent) and Italy (27.3 per cent) barely rated at all. The reason for the discrepancy can be seen in the response to Germany. Unlike the Greeks, who were our allies in World War II, the Germans had the advantage of "white" skin. The German approval rating was 55.4 per cent.

My mother came here in 1962. She might have had to choose America if the Menzies government had taken that anti-olive poll literally. But the more significant sliding door involves Arthur Sinodinos, Howard's long-time chief of staff. His mother, like mine, came to Australia after that poll was ignored. Without Arthur's advice, John Howard might well have been a oncer.

Immigration, like deregulation, was only accepted after many years of trial, error, adaptation and reconfiguration. We can score the 1940s and '50s, and the 1980s and '90s, as glory days for public policy because community prejudices and vested interests were confronted. While Menzies did not have much time for polls in his day, handled carefully they can assist the cause of reform. Bob Hawke and Paul Keating used polling to target marginal seats and to sharpen their arguments, but they never deferred to their pollster. The advisers they looked up to were the policy wonks.

"I would have been laughed out of court if I tried to overturn policy," says Rod Cameron, Labor's federal pollster from 1974 to 1990. "Could you imagine my going to Keating and saying, 'Look, the very thing you stand for, I'm sorry it's not testing all that well, you've got to drop it'?

You would have had white-boards thrown at you if you asked him to overturn the float of the dollar."

The Hawke and Keating governments did face almost unbearable pressure from Labor's blue-collar base to slow the reform process. Ahead of the 1990 election, as interest rates peaked at 17 per cent, Bob Hawke toyed with the idea of a mortgage-relief scheme. There is no question that it would have been popular, but would the government have received any credit for it? Paul Keating told Hawke that voters would see the money as an admission that Labor had hurt them and that it no longer had faith in its own policies. Hawke dropped the idea, and won the election.

After Keating took the Labor leadership, the ACTU and most of his caucus wanted a tariff freeze. Again Keating would have none of it, although he did make a faux concession to protection by saying that his tariff cuts weren't as extreme as John Hewson's.

Labor likes to blame John Howard for allowing the polls to infect the governing bloodstream, but Kim Beazley was a willing adapter in the 1990s. The then Opposition leader was happy to let the polls do his thinking for him because for most of Howard's first two terms they showed Labor in front. Beazley was right about the unpopularity of the Howard government, but he misread its symptom – the rise of Pauline Hanson's One Nation protest party – as Labor's cue to disown the reform cause. The Hansonites were seeking something neither side could deliver: the restoration of protection, the reduction of the Asian immigration intake and the removal of assistance to indigenous Australians. Beazley tried to appease these voters with an anti-GST crusade. The strategy almost worked until Howard shook his fist at boatpeople in 2001, which was the emotional play that returned the Hansonites to the Coalition.

The critical test of leadership, always, is whether the national interest is compromised in the search for voters. I believe Howard damaged Australia by using asylum seekers as political pawns. But he didn't extend the meanness of spirit to the regular immigration program. On the contrary,

Howard became a big Australia prime minister. Immigration is the defining issue in the battle of wills between politicians and the polls, because voters, if given the chance, will always prefer fewer new arrivals. The temptation to follow the electorate was resisted by both sides of politics for sixty-five years, so what transpired in 2010 demands careful scrutiny.

Howard can argue with some justification that he never allowed the argument about border protection to pollute the regular immigration program. The same cannot be said of Julia Gillard or Tony Abbott.

Howard, of course, wasn't always for a big Australia. In 1988 he suggested that Asian immigration be slowed in the interests of social cohesion. But the Labor government he faced back then knew what it stood for. Bob Hawke snarled every time the Coalition looked like breaking the bipartisan agreement on immigration. He met the argument, called out the intolerance, and split his opponents. Howard paid for his anti-Asian comments with his job in 1989. Andrew Peacock suffered in the 1990 election campaign for trying to sneak race back onto the agenda by opposing the so-called multi-function polis.

Paul Keating, likewise, stood his ground on reconciliation, and the moral investment he made through the Redfern speech, and then the *Mabo* native-title legislation, paid out handsomely for Kevin Rudd a decade later when he made the apology to the Stolen Generations. Simon Crean, and before him Arthur Calwell, would make the same point about opposing the wars in Iraq and Vietnam. There will always be times when Labor has to take a short-term hit in the polls to reaffirm its values. Otherwise its base drifts to a none-of-the-above party such as the Greens.

"It is not as if asylum seekers just became an issue," Rod Cameron says. "I had an issue of exactly the same dimension when Joh [Bjelke-Petersen] was running for PM [in 1987]. He was running around the country saying the Japs were taking the show over, and I said to people I reported to, 'This is a big problem. Here's a way if you present the argument this way, people might say, oh, there are two sides to this.' My advice was never to ignore the problem, but to face up to it."

Howard realised that he mucked up on Asian immigration in the late 1980s, but he took his time converting to the cause. A sluggish economy was his excuse to cut the intake in his first term, and the declaration of war on boatpeople at the end of his second term appeared to seal his reputation as a small-Australia prime minister. Then he changed, remarkably, and switched the colour of the immigration program from olive to yellow and brown. The numbers Howard decided to bring here in his final two terms made many on his own side wince, but it was the correct call. Australia had the world's fastest population growth rate when the global financial crisis hit in 2008. Take Howard's immigrants out of the equation and a recession would have been more likely. One of the things that set our economy apart from those of the United States and the United Kingdom was the behaviour of the property market. While their house prices collapsed – creating a vicious cycle of mortgage stress, reduced spending and job losses – large-scale immigration kept our house prices rising because supply was lagging demand. Ordinarily shortages would be read as a case of market failure, and they are. But they also played a valuable role in maintaining the confidence of Australian households to keep consuming while the rest of the developed world turned turtle.

The polls told Gillard and Abbott that voters had forgotten about the global financial crisis. They were more worried about congestion, about asylum seekers, about any darn thing really. Only a true leader would take these complaints to their logical conclusion and propose that Australia should shrink. And this is the point where the 2010 election troubled me. The first week of the campaign found both sides agreeing to something which no previous main party leader had suggested, and which no serious policy adviser would put their name to: reducing immigration when the economy is booming.

As one of the regulars on my blog pointed out: "Another 'Ah ha' moment. Both Gillard and Abbott agree that they want to stop people like them coming to this country. Good idea!"

Gillard was born in Barry, Wales, in 1961 and migrated to Australia at the age of four. Baby Julia had problems with her lungs and their family doctor suggested the Gillards move to a warmer climate. "So we came to Australia," her mother, Moira, told the ABC's *Australian Story*.

Abbott was born in London in 1957. His parents returned to Australia in 1960. "[His] first memory is of the steam train that took them from London to Southampton, where they boarded the SS *Oronsay* for the six-week voyage to his new country," his biographer, Michael Duffy, wrote. That makes him a boatperson like my father, who took the ship from Greece to Australia in 1950.

Howard laughs when asked to comment on Gillard's sustainable Australia:

> Sustainable was her word for saying, "I'm now embracing the Opposition's policy on asylum seekers." We had a policy, it was tough on asylum seekers, I accept that. It wasn't popular with some people, it was popular with a lot of other people. But one of the things it did facilitate was a sharp increase in support in the community for orthodox immigration.

Many on the Labor side were uncomfortable with Gillard's Sydney-led race to the bottom on immigration. I had a number of big names prepared to dump on their party in the event that Labor lost the election. Sadly for this essay, the discipline of the hung parliament has zipped their lips. But the more revealing critic is Howard. It may burn Labor people to know that he has the most coherent argument against their poll-driven contortions:

> I very strongly believe that most Australians support a reasonably big immigration program providing it is for the benefit of the country. Most people look back on the last thirty or forty years and say that's been one of the good things we have done. It's been one of the big things that this country has achieved and it has been by and large bipartisan. Chifley started it, and Menzies continued it.

Howard isn't surprised that Labor turned the other way. The former

New South Wales premier Bob Carr has been "against a large immigration intake quite unrelated to prejudice – he just thinks the place is overloaded." But Howard thinks the attitudes of Carr and Gillard threaten the national interest:

> Sure, in any country you are going to have infrastructure problems and all of that, but it has been such a good thing for Australia I would hate to see us lapsing into, or embracing, an attitude that does damage to the country. I thought Julia Gillard's utterances didn't seem to be the product of any long-term thinking or philosophy or whatever. They just seemed to be opportunistic.

Ouch.

But the same observation could be made of Abbott. In fact, it was the Opposition leader who first decided to play politics with the intake even though he was a supporter of a big Australia. In January 2010, as debate raged over the bashing of Indian students in Victoria, Abbott gave a speech calling for tolerance:

> Since 1970, an Australia that's four times richer has more than coped with a population that's two times greater. My instinct is to extend to as many people as possible the freedom and benefits of life in Australia. A larger population will bring that about provided that it's also a more productive one.

Yet a couple of months later he changed his position when he saw an opportunity to wedge Labor. By the election campaign, he was promising to reduce the intake by the end of a first term of Coalition government, regardless of economic conditions. If the definition of political cowardice is to turn against one's own publicly stated values because of the polls, then Abbott's stance on immigration is no better than Rudd's was on climate change.

Stop the boats – and close the immigration desk at the airport. Howard never made the link between border protection and the regular immigration program. In this he was merely continuing the bipartisan tradition on immigration that began with Ben Chifley and Robert Menzies. And on border protection, his position was really not that much different from Labor's – Keating had introduced mandatory detention, Howard had introduced offshore processing. The argument by the 2010 election was where, not whether. Labor claimed to have the more humane policy because it wanted asylum seekers interned in East Timor, a signatory to the UN convention, rather than on Nauru.

Abbott broke the seal on the regular program by joining the dots from the boats to the immigration numbers to the population debate. Gillard had a choice. She could have drawn on the Hawke example and called Abbott out for playing with the national interest. But she reached, instead, for a dog whistle of her own, the notion of a sustainable Australia.

No self-respecting leader would believe that public opinion is sufficiently informed to set the immigration intake. The numbers rise and fall from year to year depending on demand for labour. To cut when employers can't find enough skilled workers is to dare the Reserve Bank to raise interest rates to place a lid on wages. To tell China and India, the main customer for our quarry and a major supplier of our immigrants, that Australia isn't interested in offering their best and brightest a home any-more is to invite a belly-laugh across the Pacific. The Americans may be down on their knees at the moment, but their national survival instinct compels them to continue increasing their population. If we don't want them, they'll have them.

I'm prepared to argue that Australia is better off putting the people ahead of the services, and taking the risk of straining the environment in the short term, because the demands that come with a large intake are more likely to force governments to provide those services, and look after the environment over the longer term. Slowing population growth reduces our national income. It also excuses state governments from building new schools and hospitals, and reforming their planning codes to increase and improve the housing stock. As an example, just look at what happened to

New South Wales over the past decade, when its population growth, and gross state product, lagged behind the rest of the nation. Congestion wasn't eased – in fact, it became worse – because Labor downed tools.

We should be expanding the immigration program to mine the youth belts of the United States, the United Kingdom and continental Europe. The time to grab these people is while their economies are on the mat. Pay their airfares if need be! It would be no different from the transaction that brought the Gillards to Australia in the mid-1960s. Forty years from now, our first American-born prime minister might look back at her mother country and say she wouldn't be a Yank for quids.

The business case for immigration often gets more publicity than it deserves because it is couched in the cost-benefit language of economic rationalism: you should accept these people because they will pay well above the reserve for your house. The better argument is the one that Chifley and Menzies made together after World War II: that we need more people to secure Australia. The threat today is not invasion, but ageing. Australia is one of only a handful of First World societies that can stay relatively young by keeping its doors open. Immigration doesn't reverse ageing, but it does slow it.

Gillard and Abbott offered no evidence to support their argument to shrink Australia, only polls.

*

So when did polling gain the right of veto over policies such as immigration and climate change? Federal Labor acquired the disease from its New South Wales division, according to a number of sources. The carriers were the New South Wales senator Mark Arbib and his ally Karl Bitar, who became Labor national secretary after the 2007 election.

Simon Crean puts it more diplomatically. I asked him how many in the parliament today are interested in policy. "I would say it is still more about policy in the House of Representatives. [But] it has been about politics in the Senate for some considerable time."

The ad man who came up with the "Kevin 07" label, Neil Lawrence, says Arbib and Bitar have taken research too far:

> It's clear, and there is probably a majority consensus, that the turning point for Kevin Rudd was him walking away from the ETS. Real pressure advice was brought to bear from the national secretariat – from Bitar and his parliamentary compatriot Arbib – on the basis of polling and focus-group work.

Lawrence says polling took on a talismanic power. What the disengaged said in focus groups became policy because Arbib and Bitar were often able to convince Rudd and others that this was the last word in a debate:

> I think there was increasing deference paid to the polls in the Rudd prime ministership, [as] witnessed by the reversal on one of the three issues that he won the election on, that he had spoken so strongly about in terms we were all familiar with. I think it is self-evident the power that these things have come to wield.

Done properly, focus-group research can still act as an early warning device, alerting governments to the issues they need to keep talking about if they want to turn public opinion their way. But governments must be sure of their own beliefs before they go polling; they can't look to the electorate for advice on what to stand for. To read the polls as a cheat-sheet on what not to say, as Rudd and Gillard did, was to confuse means with ends.

Rod Cameron says Labor simply hasn't moved with the times:

> They are still using the Cameron formula, which was repeat, repeat, repeat the message, and when you are sick of it, repeat it some more. The assumption was voters will only ever see it once because they only get their political information on the Channel Nine news. That was true twenty or thirty years ago, but now [it's not].
>
> The other idea was [to] feed back to them what they say in the focus groups. Now that really worked for a decade, but that doesn't

work anymore. They are awake to spin, they are ahead of the game,
and they get their political information from a plethora of sources.
So there is a lot more political noise at the water cooler.

Technology has allowed political professionals to collect more information. The mistake they made was to assume all that extra data brings them closer to understanding what is in a voter's heart. I suspect the impulses to xenophobia and greed, the fear of outsiders and the desire for middle-class welfare, are over-amplified by polling techniques that ask people what they don't like and what they want. Voters can identify problems, but they expect leaders to solve them, or at least to explain why things are the way they are.

The medium has overwhelmed all else. Polling dominates the thinking of government and the media in almost equal measure. The range of numbers, and the rapidity with which they are updated, undermines a leader even when he or she is in front because any result below their best can be taken as a rebuke.

The newspaper opinion polls – Newspoll, ACNielsen, Galaxy – have become the cheapest form of content for a political reporter. No need to pick up the phone, just pull out the latest table and type. How is the government travelling? Is Brendan Nelson the most unpopular Opposition leader in history? Gee, look at the undecideds on the mining tax – do they know something we don't?

We've been living with poll-sourced volatility for two decades now. Arguably the first Opposition leader to lose his job with the assistance of the published polls was John Howard in 1989. The Bulletin had famously called him "Mr 17 per cent" and asked why he bothered. Between 1989 and 1991, there were three Opposition leaders – Howard, Andrew Peacock and John Hewson – and two prime ministers – Bob Hawke and Paul Keating. Recession can explain part of the churn in this period. What followed, though, was a form of perpetual crisis that bore no relationship to the economic cycle.

I know I'm whistling in the wind, but wouldn't it be nice if Newspoll were to go back to one poll per month? The *Australian*'s survey of federal voting intentions went fortnightly in 1992 and Newspoll made its reputation in the following year's election by picking the late swing to Labor. Don't change what works, right? Unfortunately, two Newspolls per month throughout a term provide too much temptation for mischief. Every half-smart backbencher can pull together a spreadsheet to show why their boss should be rolled. Lobby groups just have to wait for a couple of bad polls before they put the squeeze on government.

It may be a coincidence, of course, but there has been a dizzying turnover of political leadership talent since Newspoll went fortnightly. The Liberals were the first Opposition to have three leaders in a term between 1993 and 1996. The man in the middle, Alexander Downer, was the first major-party leader not to contest a federal election. On the Labor side, Simon Crean was pulled down at the end of 2003, before he could face the people in the following year. Labor also had three leaders between 2004 and 2007. But these were mere dress rehearsals for the chaos of the past three years, when a first-term government had two prime ministers and a first-term Opposition had three leaders. The trend is clearly accelerating.

The trigger shifts with the circumstances. It may be the two-party vote that drives the coup, or it may be the preferred prime minister rating. It doesn't matter which number is highlighted, because an incumbent under siege has no counter to the accumulated weight of Newspoll. Even a rogue poll – the one in twenty that is outside the margin of error – can play a part. Newspoll had one apparent rogue in each of the past two terms. Instead of being brushed off as too extreme to be taken seriously, the survey sent the incumbent into a panic. Howard got his in the middle of the APEC leaders' meeting in Sydney in September 2007. Labor's two-party vote had jumped 4 per cent to an inconceivable 59 per cent. Howard asked Downer, his foreign minister, to take soundings on whether he should stand down as prime minister. The next survey found the Labor vote back to where it had been before the blip, at 55 per cent. Howard was able to assure his colleagues that he had made up ground during the crisis.

Rudd's turn came in November 2009, when Newspoll slashed an unusually high Labor vote by 7 per cent to 52 per cent. He assumed the trigger was the increasing numbers of boatpeople that were making a dash for Australia's prosperous shores. I suspect Rudd had forewarning that a bad poll was coming, because on the night before it was published he did five radio interviews in an hour and then appeared on the ABC's 7.30 *Report*. The next Newspoll had Labor's two-party vote back at 56 per cent. Nothing had happened in the real world, but in the hall of polling mirrors Rudd had telegraphed his insecurity.

Perhaps little harm is done if a leader wastes his or her time making too many media appearances. But it becomes a concern for public policy when the prime minister brings out the chequebook to influence a single survey. In mid-February 2010, Newspoll found the Coalition had edged ahead of Labor on the primary vote, but still trailed 52 per cent to 48 per cent after preferences. Rudd made nine announcements in a fortnight, from 17 February, the day after that poll came out, to 1 March, the day before the next one was to be published. From mental health to counter-terrorism, from new road funding to the wind-up of the insulation program, the nine announcements betrayed a loss of perspective. By this stage Rudd had rejected the advice to call an early double-dissolution election on climate change. If there is a moment in history when a leader allowed himself to be bluffed by an opinion poll when he was in front, this was it.

I checked to see when Newspoll assumed its omnipotence in political reporting and political decision-making. It was more recently than I had anticipated. In the three months before the calling of the 2001 election, the *Australian* published forty-six articles that mentioned Newspoll. Ahead of the 2004 election, it was fifty-two articles, so no discernible change. But it jumped to 167 in 2007, and in the final three months of Rudd's prime ministership it was 161. That's almost two stories a day on average. (My name is on a few of those, I confess.)

The *Australian* no longer just publishes a report of the fortnightly poll and an accompanying analysis. The results are cross-referenced in all sorts of stories. Every other media organisation covers Newspoll as well. The film writer Michael Bodey tells me it is the same with movies. Box-office takings have become a standard point of reference. The question is not "Is this film worth seeing?" or "How was it made?" but rather "Look what it made."

Newspoll has created a self-fulfilling cycle of anticipation, interpretation, rejection and impatience for the next instalment. Best not tell the political junkies, but the polling the media uses is less reliable now than it was in the 1990s. An election-shaping segment of population, Generation Y, can't be surveyed because it only uses mobile phones. The internet has complicated the market further; any firm can do a quickie poll online, increasing the risk of dodgy data getting into the mainstream news media.

Rudd lived and died by the polls, just as Howard did before him. When they were up, these socially awkward men felt invincible. No one in the party room dared speak out against them. As for the public servants, well, they were on performance contracts, so they could read the polls just like anyone else.

But when the trend-line moved against these leaders, they were forced to make exaggerated gestures of contrition. Rudd appeared on the ABC's *Insiders* at the end of his announcement spree in February 2010 and addressed the polls as if they were the nation itself:

> We are taking a whacking in the polls now. I'm sure we'll take an
> even bigger whacking in the period ahead. And the bottom line is,
> I think we deserve it, both not just in terms of recent events, but
> more broadly.

The published polls are a security blanket for political journalists, just as the private ones are for the main parties. We have poll-driven columnists tut-tutting at poll-driven politicians. Polls create a false sense of precision in what is an imperfect science. Yet politics is a contact sport, between leader and community. Those who rely on polling forget that voters know they are being watched, and manipulated.

The juvenile tone of the 2010 election campaign was set by the Labor Party feud that preceded it. Not the 23 June confrontation between Kevin Rudd and Julia Gillard that saw the latter take the former's job, but Bob Hawke versus Paul Keating. Like two old bulls who didn't know when to stop charging, they tore through Gillard's election preparations with a dramatic escalation of their twenty-year public spat. Neither man would have meant any disrespect, but they seemed to catch the zeitgeist by forgetting that Gillard was about to face the people as the nation's first female prime minister.

Keating had read a part of Hawke's new biography by his wife, Blanche d'Alpuget. He thought the extract belittled his own achievements as treasurer, and wrote an angry three-page letter, which was hand-delivered to Hawke's Sydney office and then published on the front page of the *Australian*:

> This letter is written now, not simply to express my disappointment but to let you know that enough is enough. That yours and Blanche's rewriting of history is not only unreasonable and unfair, more than that, it is grasping. It is as if, Narcissus-like, you cannot find enough praise to heap upon yourself.

Gillard wouldn't take sides: "They are two great Australians having a passionate discussion about their politics. And I have to say as someone with an intense interest in politics, I am enjoying it."

As soon as Hawke and Keating were done, other former leaders would hijack the campaign itself. Rudd was the passive-aggressive father at the wedding, sending death stares to the daughter as she gave her reception speech. He invited the media to his local campaign events, then said nothing. When the leaking commenced against Gillard, he continued to say nothing. It was only after the polls showed Labor headed for defeat that Rudd became a team player again. But even then his body language betrayed him: he wouldn't give his leader the courtesy of looking at her during their stage-managed strategy meeting to assure voters they were on the same side.

Mark Latham was the mad uncle at the wedding who hijacked the microphone to tell the guests that love sucked and they should all go home. He took to the campaign trail to confront Gillard in a stunt that reflected poorly on him and the Nine Network. It's a moot point whether either man would have tried to crowd out a fellow male leader.

If you pit the recent past, Rudd and Latham, against Hawke and Keating, the source of Labor's 21st-century crisis is obvious. Rudd and Latham flew solo as leaders. They shared the loner's intolerance of their workmates. No one in the caucus was as good as they were, so they felt they had to do everything for themselves. Latham's 2004 election tilt was the training run for Rudd's government of one. Once their respective stints as leader faltered, each found they had no one watching their back. Latham resigned and Rudd was torn down. Then they turned on their colleagues without regard for the party they served. Rudd denies he had anything to do with the leaks that sent Gillard's campaign into the ditch, but someone close to him felt strongly enough about his departure to risk destroying a first-term Labor government.

By contrast, Hawke and Keating were grown-ups and party loyalists in government. They kept a lid on their personal rivalry for three successful terms that remade Australia. The public sensed that they had fallen out, but still re-elected them in 1990, and gave Keating a term in his own right after he toppled Hawke in 1991. The argument between these two giants is about who deserves the greater credit for what economists and political scientists around the world agree is the Australian miracle.

It is pathetic, of course, because the partnership was more important than the contribution of either individual. Hawke held the nation together and Keating made sure the policies added up and explained it all with memorable phrases. You couldn't have one without the other. But there is substance behind the bitterness.

Hawke's star shines brighter today with the hindsight of Howard and

Rudd's centralisation of power. Hawke was blessed with a talented cabinet. The economic hardheads, most notably Keating, Ralph Willis, John Dawkins and Peter Walsh, gave the government its spine. The spending ministers, including Brian Howe and Neal Blewett, delivered innovative policies that respected both sides of the budget. Gareth Evans excelled as foreign minister and Kim Beazley starred as defence minister. None of these Labor heroes would have tolerated a micromanaging prime minister any more than it would have occurred to Hawke to try to tell them what their line of the day would be when they fronted the media.

Ministers were given free rein over their portfolios. Keating only wore two big defeats in his eight years as treasurer. Hawke denied him a consumption tax in 1985, which was probably the right political call. And he denied him again on telecommunications reform in 1990, when Keating wanted the old Telecom split up and exposed to full competition. Hawke got that one wrong, and the consequences of his veto are still being felt two decades later as Labor tries to separate Telstra's network and retail arms through the back door of the national broadband network.

Where Hawke and Keating excelled was in the manner in which they debated issues. Discussion papers preceded the release of important announcements so that the public had time to chew over the detail of reform. Trade-offs were routine. New taxes on capital gains and fringe benefits were offset by cuts to the top personal tax rate and the removal of the double taxation of shares. Real wages were held down to improve the profitability of business in return for increases in the social wage, including free health through Medicare and universal superannuation. There was a shared sense of mission with the press gallery, which enjoyed the joust on serious topics.

Lobby groups did complain often, and the media did run interference. The assets test on the age pension pitted the Hawke government against the Herald and Weekly Times before Rupert Murdoch reclaimed his father's company. But Hawke and Keating persisted. The public backdowns, like Keating's defeats in cabinet, could be counted on one hand.

Hawke never felt the need to prove himself against his ministers, as Rudd and Latham did with their much less intimidating ministries and shadow ministries. Hawke encouraged his staff just as much as he did his ministers, and looked up to his economics adviser, Professor Ross Garnaut, who was a key backer of the float of the dollar. A generation later, Garnaut would write the report on climate change for Rudd. But the prime minister preferred the advice of his pollsters to that of Garnaut.

Here is the other rub for the present generation of politicians: Keating didn't move against Hawke when the polls were bad. Keating wrote in his 2010 letter that he carried Hawke for four years through an "emotional and intellectual malaise" between 1984 and 1988. Most of his colleagues disputed the time-frame, but not the essence of his point: that he defended Hawke, even when they didn't get along. Keating wrote:

> No other prime minister could have survived going missing for that long. But with my help, you were able to. Kevin Rudd had two months of bad polls and you were the first to say he should be replaced.

In the days before the polling tail wagged the policy dog, governments assumed unpopularity as a necessary burden of office. They would have a tough budget in year one, deal with the unexpected in the second year, then, provided there was no last-minute incompetence, devote the third year of a term to re-election.

The power of the Hawke–Keating model was that their reforms won them credit with the electorate. It was a testament to tough love. The public said they hated each measure, but no Labor government before or since has been able to win five consecutive elections. Hawke won the fourth with interest rates at 17 per cent. Keating claimed the fifth with unemployment at 11 per cent. The magic rubbed off on John Howard, who won a second term by selling a GST at a time when unemployment was at 8 per cent.

Hawke and Keating entered public life at the end of the long post-war boom. Hawke became ACTU president in 1970, the year after Keating was first elected to parliament. Like Howard, who arrived in 1974, they believed that the only way to rebuild a sense of national purpose was to expose the economy to competition.

By contrast, the three Liberal leaders since the fall of the Howard government are all members of what I will term "the prosperity generation" – political beneficiaries of Australia's longest boom. Tony Abbott entered parliament in a by-election in 1994. Brendan Nelson was part of the conservative landslide of 1996. Malcolm Turnbull arrived in 2004.

On the Labor side are Rudd and Gillard, who were part of the 1998 intake. Before them there was Latham, who joined the club at the same time as Abbott.

The character trait that links this group, and the times in which they serve, is impatience. Latham lasted thirteen months as Labor leader before quitting altogether. Nelson was ousted after nine months as Liberal leader. His pushy successor, Turnbull, had fifteen months before he was knifed by Abbott. Rudd couldn't manage a full term as Labor prime minister. Gillard ran the government for three weeks before rushing to the polls.

A few months, a year at best, then back in the dole queue. Not enough time to master the craft, but more than enough to demonstrate your unsuitability. It would be unfair to call any of them flaky, yet this sextet is representative of a bipartisan decline.

What intimidates them are the metrics of voting intentions and personal ratings, and an unforgiving electorate. The voters, who can be hypocritical at the best of times, refuse to give leaders the chance to learn from their mistakes: one blunder and they are gone.

The prosperity generation did observe the odd crisis, but the danger would pass before the next Newspoll came out. The Asian financial meltdown didn't affect us in 1997–98. The US-sourced tech wreck of 2000–01 didn't make it here either. And the big one, the global recession of 2008–09, exempted just one Western economy: ours. Each escape would remind the prosperity generation that the Australian model worked, so there was no urgency to update it. The esoteric challenges of the future could always wait until after another election victory had been secured.

Deregulation meant government had less to do. With nothing at stake, the prosperity generation exaggerated the trivial. Latham played the SNAG card by asking Howard why his government didn't support reading to children. Rudd promised to monitor petrol and grocery prices to prove he was a better economic manager than Howard. Nelson dared Rudd to cut fuel excise by five cents a litre. Turnbull accused Rudd of corruption because he accepted a second-hand ute from a Brisbane car dealer. Gillard and Abbott promised to crack down on young hoodlums carrying knives. The phoney crises blur after a while. You keep expecting one or other combatant to wink at the camera to let the voter know they are putting on a show. But they mean it, every day, because the world ends for them if they don't win that day's media.

There was one more problem. The prosperity generation of politicians was drawn from a narrower gene pool just as the nation was becoming more diverse. Eight years separated John Button's *Quarterly Essay, Beyond Belief,* in 2002, and Rodney Cavalier's book *Power Crisis,* published immediately after the 2010 election. Button, another of the ministerial stars of the Hawke and Keating governments, compared the backgrounds of the MPs who came to power in the Hawke government with those of the Beazley Opposition. The first Hawke ministry had "a pretty good social mix":

> [It included] former farmers, businessmen, academics, lawyers and union officials, as well as a former engine driver, a teacher, a retailer, a waterside worker and a shearer. The government that reformed and deregulated the economy was not made up of political mandarins.
>
> Yet look at what a cloistered profession the parliamentary Labor Party has become. After Kim Beazley's vigorous campaign in the 1998 election, Labor returned to parliament with a party of 96 members of vastly changed occupational backgrounds. Although

one medical practitioner, one public servant and one engineer remained, no farmers or tradesmen did. There were two academics, two teachers and nine lawyers, but the social complexion had changed. What had replaced a broad spectrum of backgrounds was a new class of political operator who had been filtered through the net of ALP machine politics. Out of the 96 members, 53 came from jobs in party or union offices. These members described themselves variously as "administrators," "officials" and "electoral officers." There were also 10 former members of state parliaments and nine described as political consultants, advisers and lobbyists.

Cavalier, a former New South Wales Labor minister in the 1980s, deals with the disintegration of the state government over the issue of electricity privatisation. But the condition he describes applies across the party:

> Inside one generation, the catchment for parliamentary prefer-
> ment is increasingly restricted to those who work on the staff of a
> minister, in the ALP office or an affiliated union … The political
> class has captured the Labor Party in parliament and the machine.
> Its knowledge of Labor history and respect for Labor's traditions is
> zero; sub-zero really, as contempt for branches and the old ways
> is a staple of conversation.

*

The dividing line between the reform and the digital eras is the goods and services tax (GST), the last significant piece of policy that was pursued in defiance of the opinion polls. History records this as a decisive win for Howard, but the lesson he drew from it was, "Never again." I place Howard with a foot in each camp. The early Howard continued the Hawke–Keating project; late Howard wrote the manual for trivial government.

The GST almost killed Howard because he couldn't adequately compensate pensioners and self-funded retirees. They were his base, the over-fifties, and they had signed his political death notice twice before, first in the run-up to the 1998 election, before the GST package was released, and then ahead of the 2001 election, as tax reform was being digested by the community. The sequence is worth recalling because it set the dominoes tumbling for the rest of the decade, from the war on boatpeople to the use of government as an automated teller machine to buy off aggrieved voters.

Howard had found himself in the same first-term hole that Rudd fell into, with the Coalition primary vote at 34 per cent at the end of June 1998. But it never occurred to Liberal MPs to swap leaders before the election, then only three months away.

"At the time I don't think the deputy [Peter Costello] was as popular as she [Gillard] is now, I think that's the difference," Arthur Sinodinos told me on the day Gillard replaced Rudd. Looking back on the Coalition's first-term blues, Sinodinos said the government held together despite the polls because there was a unity of purpose in the cabinet. "They knew that their best chance of getting back was to have something to fight for, and that's where tax reform and the GST came in."

Howard needed the tax package to show he had a plan for a second term. Without it, both sides agree, he would have been a oncer. The government prevailed despite the loss of nineteen seats to Labor and a swing of 4.6 per cent against it.

The 1998 election proved to be a false dawn for Labor and its first-term Opposition leader, Kim Beazley. Victory had very nearly been achieved with a simple message: stop the GST. Labor anticipated that the GST would be an impossible tax to implement without hurting voters, so it bet the next campaign on the same issue. No introspection or policy reappraisal was deemed necessary, other than to disown the excesses of the Keating government; Labor relied on the polling that told it the GST was rat poison.

The Australian Democrats had campaigned for the GST, but with food exempted. But Howard wasn't interested in a half-baked GST while the Tasmanian independent senator Brian Harradine was still talking. In May 1999, however, Harradine declared he could not support the new tax. Howard was stunned. He thought about sending the issue straight back to the people through a double-dissolution election. Instead he swallowed his pride and opened negotiations with the Democrats.

The parallel with the emissions trading scheme is fascinating. Kevin Rudd refused to compromise with the Greens after the Coalition blocked the ETS legislation in December 2009. He too passed up the opportunity of a double-dissolution election.

Rudd would have recalled that Howard was a reluctant negotiator with the Democrats. He agreed to their demands on food, and had to whittle back the tax cuts for higher-income earners to pay for the exemption. It represented 80 per cent of the original package, but Howard reasoned it was better than no GST at all.

"It would have been seen as a massive loss for Howard, after having won the election on this thing by the skin of his teeth that he couldn't get the thing through," Sinodinos says. "I think it would have finished his leadership and would have allowed Peter Costello to come up."

I spoke to Howard after the 2010 election. He said he never thought of the GST dilemma in terms of his own job. But he did concede the point that backing down would have rebounded on him:

> I don't know that I sat down and thought through what the implica-
> tions for my leadership were. I just knew it would be very bad for
> the government if we had walked away from the GST, and some-
> thing that is bad for the government is always bad for the boss.

The GST suffered teething problems in late 2000 and early 2001, which set off a chain reaction in the polls. The Coalition lost state elections in Queensland and Western Australia, and the federal seat of Ryan in Brisbane's leafy west in a by-election. On paper, Howard was in worse shape than he had been in 1998. He responded by sending the budget into deficit for one year to buy off the defectors. But only after saying he wouldn't compromise.

"I cease to be of any value to the Australian people if I do things that I don't believe in because of political pressure, and the Australian people will not respect me for that," Howard declared, a fortnight before buckling to the motor lobby. That handout, which abolished automatic indexation of the fuel excise, marked the formal end of the reform era. The motor lobby had only asked for a one-off 1.5-cents-a-litre reduction as compensation for the GST. Howard gave them more because he fretted that Labor might gazump him. It was not the way Hawke and Keating had done things. But it was the way Malcolm Fraser had governed between 1975 and 1983. Hawke and Keating were the leaders out of the box, and the passage of time has only made their governments appear more bold.

The fuel excise hand-out plays tricks with the memory of those on the conservative side. Howard's advisers who opposed it say it worked to kill a political problem. Yet the gesture didn't help the government in the polls: two months after it was announced, the Coalition's primary vote was back at 35 per cent. Howard needed another round of hand-outs to older voters, which were announced in the May 2000 budget, to stabilise the conservative base.

The nation's coffers are $6 billion a year poorer today without indexation. Double that cost for the removal of food from the GST, and you get an idea why no debate about tax reform in the future can proceed without another go at strengthening the indirect tax base to take the weight off personal income tax.

The GST exhausted Howard. It was one of those double-edged arguments where the media claimed the high ground of righteousness at the expense of good policy. We goaded the prime minister into adopting the GST after the 1996 election, then gave him grief on the detail even though he had won a mandate for tax reform in 1998. He said there would be no losers, so we screamed "gotcha" each time he was a decimal point shy of the perfection he promised.

Who could blame Howard for taking the opportunity to recast his leadership in August 2001 when a stricken boat of mainly Afghani asylum seekers rescued at sea by the Norwegian vessel the *Tampa* refused to return to Indonesia? The confrontation occurred only days before the 11 September terrorist attacks on New York and Washington. Border protection and the war against al-Qaeda were fused in the public mind for long enough to make voters forget what they thought was bothering them at the kitchen table. Howard became father figure to the nation, and then later, when the mining boom came, he added generous uncle to his persona.

Labor went into a long period of self-flagellation after the *Tampa* election. Mention boatpeople and they would curse that scoundrel Howard for allowing the redneck minority of the population to decide the circumstances in which campaigns are fought. Mention the hand-out machine and they would explode. Howard had perfected a form of cashed-up and lowest-common-denominator governing that rattled Labor's faith in the nation it wanted to serve. The mob were intolerant and greedy, Labor people often told me.

Maybe they were in the early noughties. But what never made sense was Labor's refusal to mount a counter-argument. The risk-averse model of campaigning, as Julia Gillard termed it, crept into Labor thinking in two distinct phases. First, economic policy was played down after the 1996 election, then social policy after the 2001 election. Don't mention interest rates, don't mention immigration. This allowed Howard to steal Labor's policy clothes. He convinced people that he, not Hawke and Keating, had written the nation's greatest economic hits.

Howard did nothing more on the domestic front in his third term but write cheques. He delivered the biggest expansion in middle-class welfare outside of a recession, making future reforms more difficult because there is a larger group of voters who won't want to be worse off. Howard only got back on the reform horse in his fourth, and final, term when he had control of the Senate. The temptation to avoid a repeat of the GST experience proved too great and he rushed his WorkChoices legislation into law.

A sneaky reform, dropped on the public without consultation and in breach of his election commitment to leave things as they were, it invited another community backlash. When the polls showed workers were worried about their pay and conditions, Howard reached into the show bag for another distraction. He seemed to make more announcements in his final year than in the previous ten. A takeover of the Murray–Darling, tax cuts, the Northern Territory intervention, a takeover of a single hospital in Tasmania, more tax cuts. But he had used up his Houdini credits, and WorkChoices became the main reason why the Coalition was defeated at the top of the boom in 2007.

Labor assumed the Howard method should be its method. Because Howard had given up on reform, Labor did too. Because Howard aimed at the wallet every time he suffered a wobble in the polls, Labor did too.

This is why the party that held the nation together in World War II and remade it in peacetime wasn't in any shape to be an agent of change when power finally came its way again in November 2007. Labor governed by the conservative populist manual when the nation wanted something else. It was cowed by Howard, and captured by the polls.

There is a marvellous quote about Australia from the mid-1980s that is no longer supposed to be true. Australia, the *Economist* magazine observed, "is one of the best managers of adversity the world has seen – and the worst manager of prosperity." It has been twenty years since Paul Keating declared, "This is a recession that Australia had to have." For fiscal trainspotters, the anniversary falls on 29 November 2010. What is there not to love about this country? We've had two decades without recession while the United States has had two of them in the past decade.

But the noughties was our least active decade for public policy in more than a generation. No nation should be so lucky that it delays reform indefinitely without suffering any consequences.

The last time Australia appeared to decouple from the United States was at the end of the 1960s, when they had a recession and we didn't. By 1975, we had joined them in an economic and cultural decline.

Australians simply didn't get along in the 1970s. Capital conspired when Gough Whitlam was in office, and the trade unions went on strike when Malcolm Fraser replaced him. Tax cheating became commonplace as respect for institutions crumbled. We got our national kicks when Lillee and Thommo hurled bouncers at the Poms, just as they got their kicks during the Great Depression when Harold Larwood halved Don Bradman's batting average in the Bodyline series.

History may not repeat, because the mining boom will be sending more money our way, but we have already suffered for the go-slow on reform. A leading indicator of future living standards is productivity, and Australia's effort in the noughties was its weakest since the 1970s.

Of greater concern is the precedent set by the two issues that crippled the Rudd–Gillard government: climate change and the mining boom. The debates are connected because they are globalisation's ultimate test of our temperament. The quarry is making us richer than we dared dream. Yet our customers are adding to the burden of climate change: China, in particular, is both a large emitter and a wrecker of the international push for an emissions trading scheme. Do we wait for the world and enjoy the party in the meantime? Or do we go first on the understanding that prevarication would only give the Chinese another excuse to obstruct collective action?

It shouldn't be that hard to solve the riddle because we have been here before. Australia began cutting its tariffs first, before the rest of the world, in the 1980s. If we'd waited, we'd still be waiting and the global financial crisis would have had a bullet with our name on it. By going early, Australia became match fit for the trials of globalisation. The cost of cleaning up the nation's energy sources is intimidating, but it is the next necessary step on our journey to self-reliance.

Both sides of politics understand that action delayed will eventually mean higher costs for everyone. They don't need a poll to tell them that whoever is eventually forced to place a price on emissions will have done it on less than favourable terms for themselves, and the nation, because they mucked around in the noughties.

John Howard put off a decision on climate change until the polls left him no choice. Too late, because it was this issue, along with WorkChoices, that brought Labor to power. It seems so long ago now, but at the 2007 election both sides promised an emissions trading scheme. Kevin Rudd tried to one-up the Coalition by saying he'd start his within the next term; Howard was only offering to do it by 2012.

The ETS failed in the first instance because Rudd played hard on the politics, but was too soft on the policy. He didn't cut Opposition leader Malcolm Turnbull enough slack for him to get the Liberal Party over the line. True bipartisanship involves sharing the credit for legislation. It doesn't need to be a full-blown collaboration, but the Opposition does have to feel good about its decision to jump into bed with the enemy.

Rudd didn't sell the ETS beforehand because the polls assured him that the public was onside. Then, when the legislation was being negotiated, he wanted to be both good cop and bad cop, making nice behind closed doors while attacking Turnbull in public. He thought the polls were still strong enough in late 2009 to force the Opposition into signing up for his scheme. But he was nervous about offending households and industry, so he caved in on the compensation package before anyone thought to ask.

The ETS to which Rudd and Turnbull agreed took more money from the budget to appease voters than it raised in revenue from the permits to emit carbon pollution, and the start date was pushed back a year, to 1 July 2011. A revenue-negative introduction for a reform of this scale is not necessarily bad public policy, provided it doesn't lose sight of the ultimate goal of placing a price on emissions; it is the change in relative prices that drives the investment in cleaner energy. This deal, though, was harder to sell because of its soft start.

Rudd unconsciously plagiarised both the WorkChoices Howard and the GST Howard in the way he approached reform, with too little community consultation and too much cash. He misjudged the national mood by seeking a position between the Greens and the climate-change sceptics. It was the same thinking that sent Julia Gillard on her election-campaign search for the disengaged voter in the middle. The centre doesn't constitute a majority without the believers.

Turnbull couldn't hold the Opposition together because the issue split the conservatives between believers and sceptics. He was told that he could keep his job if he blocked the government legislation, an offer he refused on principle.

The intrigue betrayed a lack of seriousness on both sides. Most of the players didn't really know what they were talking about. Rudd often stumbled when asked to explain how an ETS would work, and he failed to grasp the strategic importance of sticking to his already modified reform timetable.

The Senate defeat in December 2009 triggered a frenzy of meetings. Mark Arbib advised Rudd to call an early election for February or March. He wasn't alone in holding this view; Julia Gillard, Wayne Swan and John Faulkner were also urging Rudd to move quickly because they felt the sooner Labor went to the people, the better its chances of victory.

Faulkner was the most adamant that the election be fought on climate change. Rudd chose to wait, which turned the premise of the next round of discussions on its head.

What was lost in the subsequent recriminations was the time bomb Rudd had placed under his own leadership by procrastinating. Without an early election, the window for implementing the ETS in the next term had suddenly closed, because business would not get the year's notice that it required between the legislation's passage and the 2011 start date. This created a further complication because the ETS was already written in red ink into the budget with the hand-outs exceeding the revenue; now it had to come out of the budget. Why Rudd didn't think this through at the start of the year, before events overwhelmed him, is anyone's guess.

Asked to comment on the criticism of his role, Arbib replies: "I have been and always will be a big supporter of a price on carbon – you can't reach the greenhouse reduction targets without it." He will not discuss his private conversations with Rudd.

People close to Rudd still don't know why he baulked when one poll said he would win an early election on the ETS, then folded when another said he might lose if he didn't drop the ETS.

The question that Gillard and Swan should address as his ultimate executioners is why they thought Labor could get away with abandoning its conviction on climate change. Even so, Rudd bears ultimate responsibility: this was a leader's call, and he picked the wrong poll to take at face value.

The pollster Tony Mitchelmore says leaders who take the electorate's complaints too literally sacrifice the very thing that allows them to shape public opinion: their authority. Mitchelmore stopped doing work for federal Labor soon after it went into government. When he returned to the field to conduct focus groups for his own business last year, he detected a growing disquiet about Rudd. It wasn't issue-specific; rather, it was his government's lack of clarity that made people wonder whether they really knew him.

"In September last year, he was still rating well, but in the groups they were struggling to describe him," Mitchelmore says.

> They weren't sure who he was. Some people who did have a definition of him, their picture was very different to when they elected him. Because there was that mismatch, they assumed it was just fraudulent behaviour, he was not being genuine, it was just an act.

The ETS reversal caught those doubts and amplified them. On this the pollsters and the policy wonks agree. Ross Garnaut used a lecture during the 2010 election campaign to savage the Labor Party that used to look up to his advice:

> The position on climate change is weak only because of an extraordinary failure of leadership. The failure is a product and represents the nadir of the early 21st-century political culture, in which short-term politics and accession to sectional pressures has held sway over leadership and analysis of the national interest. Those political advisers who turned out to have greatest influence over former prime minister Rudd weighed undoubtedly strong resistance from special-interest groups, and inchoate reactions from partially informed members of the community, above more fundamental determinants of political success. They played down the unusual reality of majority support for a measure involving major structural change in the economy. More fundamentally, they ignored the crucial respect for the role of leadership in the democratic process. In accepting their advice, Kevin Rudd abdicated the leadership of Australia, and set the scene for the destruction of his prime ministership.

The Liberals were no better; they too let the polls do their thinking for them. Tony Abbott took the Opposition leadership by one vote in December 2009. He didn't expect to win until the favoured candidate, Joe Hockey, was counted out first in a three-way ballot with Turnbull.

Abbott had been a supporter of the ETS before he was against it. He said the science was "crap" but he still felt the undertow of the polls dragging him towards a gesture on climate change, so his first act as leader was to promise $3.2 billion in hand-outs over four years to buy emissions cuts.

He ran three fantastically contradictory lines. He agreed climate change was happening, while questioning the science. He said Rudd's scheme was a great big new tax on everything, even though it was revenue-negative. And he had his own budget-draining plan to buy reductions in carbon pollution from industry and farmers, while simultaneously arguing that only a Coalition government could pay back the debt and end the waste.

On releasing his "direct action" plan for climate change in February 2010, Abbott must have known the gods were smiling on him. In the reform era of the 1980s and '90s, any party that announced new spending without saying where the money was coming from would have been monstered by the media, the economics profession and business groups. Kim Beazley or Andrew Peacock would never have been allowed to get away with un-costed policies by the Howard, Keating or Hawke govern-ments. But Abbott evaded even token scrutiny, because his climate-change gesture was a one-day wonder and it was judged to be no more than a piece of political theatre.

Treasury had sharp words for both sides in the briefs it prepared for whoever won the election. The blue book for the Coalition said, cuttingly, that using the budget, rather than a market mechanism, to tackle climate change is not in the national interest. Treasury reminded the Coalition that it was already committed to reducing emissions by 5 per cent below their 2000 levels by 2020:

> [This] cannot be achieved without a carbon price unless significant economic and budget impacts are to be imposed. A broad-based market mechanism which prices carbon, driving large scale abate-ment through long-term investment in low emissions technologies and changes in behaviour by both producers and consumers across

the economy, is the only realistic way of achieving the deep cuts in emissions that are required. Market based mechanisms represent the lowest cost pathway when compared with regulation, mandatory standards or budget-financed initiatives ... Moreover, many direct action measures cannot be scaled up to achieve significant levels of abatement anyway, and for those that can be scaled up, the cost per tonne of abatement would rise rapidly, imposing further costs on taxpayers and consumers.

There is an understandable tone of frustration in the document: "Too much time has already been wasted – for which the Australian community will necessarily pay a higher price."

Defending the government's approach, Julia Gillard says that while it is easy to criticise with the benefit of hindsight, Labor nearly succeeded:

We went for a political consensus, and we almost got there. [But] because the focus was on driving that political consensus, the complex conversation with the electorate was not being had and the absence of that complex conversation showed in the election.

That the Rudd model almost worked does not redeem it. The very fact that he relied on Turnbull, who was the most passionate advocate for action in either of the main parties, meant Rudd was seeking the path of least resistance by negotiating with a believer. The more serious conversation had to be had with the public.

Dealing with climate change became more difficult after the global financial crisis hit because business wanted a breather. Rudd and Turnbull were sympathetic and settled on a package which made the transition almost pain-free for business, but that gave the Greens the excuse to sit on the sidelines when the Abbott coup overturned the bipartisan agreement.

The deference to capital is puzzling because it routinely lets down both sides of politics. The last notable example of a business-led reform debate was in 1997, when the Australian Chamber of Commerce and

Industry and the Australian Council of Social Service gave the Howard government the political cover to revive the GST. This is how the business lobby used to operate under the Hawke and Keating governments. It would argue for deregulation on the grounds of self-interest, of course, but it was really doing the government's bidding. The Business Council of Australia would start a debate to the right of Labor, giving the government room to convince its own constituencies in caucus and the trade unions to take a seemingly more moderate position. If the electorate sniffed a set-up, it didn't mind because the image of a Labor government being helped along by business suggested the national interest was driving policy.

Rudd and Turnbull gave business what it asked for, and more – just as Howard had with the motor lobby over fuel excise. The pattern of appeasement has convinced business to revert to its pre-1980s state, when it behaved like an impatient child in the lolly shop, trying to force its open hand to the front of the counter.

So if the kids get too greedy, why not punish them by taking away their allowance? You could almost hear the impulse to retribution override Rudd's diplomatic brain. He'd been so accommodating to business on the ETS and yet it wouldn't go to war for him to convince the Coalition to hold its nerve. Then he deferred to those on his side who said, "Cut your losses on the ETS," and he was punished for doing so by the polls. Well, if the people want conviction, let's try tax reform.

All the political ills of the past decade – the policy indolence, the partisan self-obsession and the bloody-mindedness – found their most toxic expression in the mining-tax debate. The rule book for reform was torn up.

Like everything Rudd took on, it was a terrific idea at the time. At the 2020 Summit, tax reform was the suggestion that had most delegates nodding. The head of Treasury, Ken Henry, was given the task of conducting a root-and-branch review of the tax and payments systems when the budget was still in surplus. Only two items were off-limits: the rate and base of the GST, and tax-free superannuation payouts.

Henry's advice to the incoming Rudd government had been the same as it had been to the Howard government: the best way to return the surplus to the public was in the form of lower taxes. All other spending proposals were not as efficient in economic terms. Interestingly, the public didn't see it that way, telling the pollsters they preferred increased spending to tax cuts.

What no one appreciated in the first half of 2008 was that our surplus was a sign of something about to explode. The global financial crisis promptly sent the budget into record deficit, as the world economy reset our income clock. The government could have pushed back the Henry review until the budget could afford it, or narrowed its scope. But Rudd being Rudd, he insisted they continue as if nothing had happened.

Tax reform and a generous increase in the age pension added to an already over-full plate. Then Rudd became distracted by problems with the home-insulation program, negotiations with the states over health reform, an arm-wrestle with Gillard and Swan over the ETS, child care and preparations for the budget. Rudd sensed he had over-committed and folded under the pressure. His public demeanour suggested he was in need of a holiday. Privately, he lost focus and allowed the work to pile up. By February 2010 his colleagues were fed up, although it was still four months before he would lose the leadership. Gillard was the last to move against him because she assumed that he would snap out of his funk in time to get back to doing what he does best: campaigning. But he wasn't ready to call the election when Gillard and others were advising him to – by August or September – because the fight with the miners had taken on a life of its own.

The mining tax was another WorkChoices moment, a complex policy dumped on the public with no warning. The industry, despite protestations to the contrary, knew what was coming and supported the concept of a profits-based tax. What it objected to was Labor's timetable, which appeared to place decision before consultation.

The Henry review and the government's initial response were released in the week before the May 2010 budget. The prime minister and treasurer worried that their tax package would be seen as too timid, and that's how it was judged by political and economic commentators, myself included. There was no warning of a brawl in those early days because the two biggest miners, BHP and Rio, were muted in their first statements.

Henry had recommended a profits-based tax on mining to replace the production-based royalties levied by the states. The industry agreed with the theory, it just didn't like the way this tax was framed.

While the government embraced the review's mining-tax proposal, it had its own ideas about how to distribute the $18 billion a year in revenue. Henry wanted mining royalties abolished, but as Labor didn't want a fight with the states, it offered the miners a refund for the royalties they had already been charged, at a cost of about $8 billion a year. Henry wanted the mining tax to fund a five-cents-in-the-dollar reduction in the company-tax rate, which would account for the remaining $10 billion in revenue. Labor settled for a two-cent cut, or $4 billion for companies, and used the other $6 billion to pay for tax breaks for small business, bank interest income, infrastructure spending and to boost the superannuation levy from 9 per cent to 12 per cent of workers' wages. The Henry review's grand bargain to transfer the proceeds of the mining boom to the rest of the economy through a reduced company-tax rate had been diluted.

A few quick points on the detail. The complaint that the resource super profits tax (or the "Aretha Franklin tax", as it was dubbed by Treasury officers because the acronym RSPT reminded them of her version of Otis Redding's song "Respect") amounted to double taxation was nonsense. Mining has always been taxed twice. The argument that mining already paid its fair share was also wrong. The Minerals Council of Australia said its members faced an above-average corporate-tax burden. Not true. On the figures the council supplied, mining enjoyed the fourteenth-lowest effective company-tax rate out of nineteen sectors. It paid a lower rate than manufacturing and construction, the very sectors it was crowding out.

The miners have been making money because their main customer, China, has inflated the world price for our coal and iron ore. A mining tax on those windfall profits poses no credible threat to the kitchen table because the Chinese wear the cost.

But the cash they send us does mess with the real economy. The mining boom soaks up every available investment dollar, and while not a big employer in its own right, the wages the resources sector is prepared to pay give every other business nightmares because its staff might want the same.

The crowding-out extends to governments, which are forced to compete with the miners for scarce labour to build roads, hospitals and schools. Royalties don't level the playing field. A profits-based tax doesn't either, but it does provide a more efficient mechanism to redistribute wealth to the rest of the economy.

The miners saw the Aretha Franklin tax as a form of nationalisation. In principle it gave taxpayers a 40 per cent stake in each mine. They collected 40 per cent of the profits above a normal rate of return, and covered 40 per cent of the losses. The miners said the guarantee on losses was worthless because no bank would lend them money on the strength of it. The government took time to concede this design flaw. It might have avoided this particular problem had it been willing to release the tax in draft form for discussion, and had the miners been prepared to engage in good-faith negotiations.

Where the government and the miners blundered together was in allowing the argument to escalate into an open advertising war. The miners were able to strong-arm the government because the prime minister had lost what his colleagues termed "the crutch of Newspoll." Even so, Rudd welcomed the brawl because he thought it would be the solution to his problem on the ETS. Show enough of his stubborn side to voters and they'd forget that he'd walked away from his principles on climate change only a month earlier. Yet Rudd's belated display of toughness came across as a prime-ministerial tantrum. Labor people were stunned when he resorted to xenophobia with the clunky observation that "these massively increased profits built on Australian resources are mostly, in fact, going overseas." They scratched their heads again when he broke his solemn promise not to use government advertising to run political campaigns.

Successful tax reforms of the past had been preceded by tax summits and discussion papers, as was the case with Paul Keating's changes in 1985. The GST package of 1998 was released after a year-long softening-up process in which the Coalition punched away at the old indirect tax system. The idea was to flush out opposition, address unintended consequences and provide the voters with sufficient information that the government had the public-relations edge over vested interests. The mining tax should have been in the public domain at least three to six months before the May budget, not one week before. That way the public focus at budget time would have been on the tax cuts associated with the reform.

Julia Gillard and Wayne Swan believe that Rudd could not have resolved this dispute before the election, and it was pivotal in their decision to move against his leadership. Rudd would disagree, but that is immaterial because he had done enough damage already in the way he conducted the tax debate.

None of this excuses what the mining industry did. To run interference against government legislation before it has been released sets an American precedent for our system, in which policy is dictated by those with the deepest pockets. The miners probably think they were just exercising their democratic right to call out a bad tax. But this was an election year, and the miners were seeking a veto no lobby is entitled to – to deny a government the right to set taxation rates. The miners wanted to destroy the tax in the court of public opinion before the government even had a chance to settle the detail in consultations with them. The place for lobbying is the parliament, where every citizen has the same theoretical right to influence the debate through their local member. If the parliament passes legislation the miners don't like, then all bets are off. Take it up with the voters at that point, as the ACTU did with its campaign against

WorkChoices. Any intervention beforehand defies a basic principle of democracy, that power is vested in the people through their parliament.

The democratic theory is one thing, but there is also a pragmatic reason why governments should never allow global firms to dictate policy. Miners have the same power as financial institutions to bring down national economies if they borrow too much. At first blush, the global financial crisis is primarily a failure of regulation and oversight. Wall Street had convinced the US government and the US Federal Reserve that the interests of the firm and the nation were the same. Leave us alone to make our billions, and we'll all be better off. Australia avoided catastrophe, in part, because our banks were well behaved and very well regulated. They still carried the scars of the 1990–91 recession when two of the big four banks almost went broke.

The big mining companies say they kept us out of the 2008–09 global recession because they continued digging while the rest of the developed world crashed. The focus groups certainly agreed with this proposition. The research had told Rudd to stop talking about the global financial crisis because the punters didn't give him credit for the effect of his government's stimulus spending. So he left a rhetorical gap that the miners were happy to fill by saying that they, not Kevin, had stepped in when the nation needed help.

With friends like these, who needs government, right? One month into the mining-tax war, Rio's chief executive officer, Tom Albanese, went on Sydney talkback radio to assert his claim to be Australia's sugar daddy.

"I want to invest in Australia, I want to put billions of capital into Australia," Albanese told Alan Jones. With his host egging him on, Albanese came close to claiming he had personally saved us.

> Albanese: Australia benefited from the mining industry –
> Jones: Absolutely.
> Albanese: – to keep these –

Jones: Absolutely.

Albanese: – the whole economy out of recession. And that helped everyone.

Jones: Yeah, I agree.

Albanese: I'd been travelling all over the world last year, in the depth of the recession, and the only place anywhere in the world where people were actually in restaurants was in Australia as they were the only ones in the world that had any money.

Jones: Good on you.

Indeed he was travelling the world in 2009. Rio was the company that almost brought the global financial crisis home to Australia when it got caught with a mountain of debt. Albanese sought to keep the banks at bay through a deal with the Chinese government. Now that was real sovereign risk, not the straw-man version the mining companies would erect in order to argue against the Aretha Franklin tax.

As the global financial crisis continues to unfold around the world, what troubles policy-makers is the prospect that a government will default on its debt. When governments default, they can either have their debts forgiven, or they can sell a bit of themselves to another nation. Rio was prepared to give Chinalco, a Chinese state-owned enterprise, the opportunity to lift its stake in the company to 18 per cent, at a fire-sale price of US$19.5 billion.

The conflict of interest was obvious to both sides of politics. Rio lobbied the Rudd government for approval. In fact, it begged, according to informed sources. Fortunately, the Chinese talked themselves out of the game by propping up the global economy. Their stimulus package put a floor under commodity prices and this allowed Rio to walk away from the deal in June 2009. The lesson of this transaction is this: beware any CEO who thinks their bottom line equals that of the nation.

In his book on the Chinese Communist Party, the journalist Richard McGregor makes a compelling case that Chinalco was not only state-owned, but state-influenced. For its part, the Chinese government insisted that the aluminum company and the party were at arm's length. McGregor writes:

> Not long after the deal collapsed, four of Rio's China-based executives were arrested in Shanghai by state security on allegations of bribery and commercial espionage. It was no wonder that political opponents of the deal in Australia were able to portray Chinalco as an agent of the state. For a Party on a mission to convince sceptics that Chinalco was an independent entity, it was another wrenching own goal.

The miners-saved-the-economy line overlooks one other important fact. Queensland, the most populous mining state, suffered the sharpest drop in state income during the global financial crisis. Queensland's gross state product grew by 0.3 per cent in 2008–09, well behind the national rate of 1.1 per cent. Only New South Wales went closer to recession, with growth of just 0.2 per cent. But New South Wales had been under-performing for a decade; this was the Sunshine State's first below-average effort in more than twenty years.

It is possible to sympathise with Rudd for wanting to poke the miners in the eye, but revenge doesn't serve the national interest either. The mining-tax debate caught all the bad habits of the past decade and packaged them into a reality TV show.

And then something funny happened on the way to the election. After Gillard replaced Rudd as prime minister, Labor's vote rebounded and the miners were suddenly keen to cut a deal, and the government was eager to give up on a few of its principles as well. Gone was the 40 per cent rate on super profits and the 40 per cent refund for losses. A 30 per cent minerals resource rent tax took its place, and it would apply to coal and iron ore only. It delivered almost as much revenue as Ken Henry's original elegant design, because the three big miners, BHP Billiton, Rio Tinto and Xstrata, had revised up their profit expectations. A lower rate on a larger pile of money seemed to satisfy both sides. But like Howard's GST deal with the Democrats, the rollback meant someone would lose a bit of their tax cut. The bunny was the non-mining business sector, which saw its company-tax cut halved by $2 billion, from two cents to one cent in the dollar. Labor would say "serves them right" for not sticking up for tax reform.

The lightning speed of the accommodation meant that the detail of the tax would have to be resolved after the election. Tony Abbott could have walked away from the fight at this stage, but he continued to oppose the tax. Like his position on climate change, it was a simple political calculation: Labor was on the nose in the mining states, so why let it off the hook even if the miners were happy?

When Rudd's polling honeymoon ended, there was no dialogue, just drama. That may have been the former prime minister's doing. Yet even Rudd's opponents in the government say the behaviour of the miners was shameless. In the non-mining business community, there was concern that the campaign had gone too far. The idea that any industry would seek to topple a government made some well-known business chiefs uncomfortable, according to a trusted conservative source. But they didn't speak out, and have no reason to do so now.

Wayne Swan says he was "disappointed by the distortions and the dishonesty encapsulated in that highly partisan but well-funded campaign":

> The truth is there was consultation, before and after the announcement, but that consultation was unfortunately coloured by big spenders like Mr Clive Palmer trying to drive a political outcome rather than a good economic outcome for the country. Australians would be far better served if arguments were won and lost on their merits and not on the basis of how much money people can afford to throw into an advertising campaign.

The treasurer says the Opposition played spoiler because it thought that would win it the election:

They are very anti-reform now. If they can't support an NBN, which is a rolled-gold case in economic theory and microeconomic reform, or a simple profits-based tax, or a boost to super in a capital-hungry nation, they have gone completely native.

The miners and the Coalition were following the lead of the trade unions. Both had seen what the ACTU achieved in John Howard's final term when it ran a national advertising blitz and a marginal-seats campaign against WorkChoices. The Liberals' federal director, Brian Loughnane, said this had never happened before:

> For the first time in our history, a third external force has intervened in our political process with resources greater than either of the major political parties. I believe this is an extremely unhealthy development. If disclosure of campaign spending is to mean anything in this country, the ACTU should be required to publish a report setting out details of how the $30 million it allocated to the campaign was spent.

Ben Chifley would beg to differ, because the banks had campaigned against their nationalisation at the 1949 election. Loughnane also forgot to mention that the Howard government spent much more than $30 million on taxpayer-funded ads to promote WorkChoices, but his point was nonetheless valid. Political parties and governments shouldn't be forced into these sorts of bidding wars. My preference would be to ban all third-party political advertising. Vested interests can make their case to journalists, who can then use that information to scrutinise government policy.

The truth is that lobby groups with more members or cash than the main parties have always had the power to thwart governments. What has changed is that labour and now capital have had a taste of the drug that is the media and polling cycle. Government has never seemed weaker, and the opportunities to intimidate it will only increase with a hung parliament.

And yet ... in mid-September 2010, days before the first sitting of the hung parliament, BHP's chief executive officer, Marius Kloppers, called for a carbon tax, a policy Gillard had explicitly ruled out for Labor's second term. This was head-spinning stuff. The mining companies had helped to bring down one Labor prime minister. Now the biggest of them all, BHP, was trying to help the new Labor prime minister find her reform voice.

Optimists would say that business and the Gillard government have taken their first tentative step towards a reform partnership. But let's see what happens when Labor gets into trouble in the polls again, or if an early election is called.

Pick a poll, any poll, in the two years when Kevin Rudd was surfing a wave of national goodwill, or in the first four weeks of Julia Gillard's prime ministership, and even the most one-eyed conservative would concede that voters were keen for Labor to succeed. To bugger it up not once but twice in the same term required a special form of political deafness on the government's behalf.

Rudd proved to be too conservative for the nation he led, while Gillard's campaign for re-election was too cynical. But the problem goes deeper than any individual's failure. Labor in office suffered a return of the identity crisis that had plagued it in its wilderness years in Opposition, when each federal defeat to John Howard would yield the same basic analysis: the party had given up its soul to the machine. In 2010 the electorate got it right by taking away Labor's majority, while at the same time leaving Gillard just enough wriggle room to secure minority government. The alternative, a return to Coalition rule after just one term in the sin bin, would have made little sense without an agenda. And let's be frank: Tony Abbott had no policies to speak of that addressed the challenges facing the nation. He thought climate change wasn't real enough to warrant action, and that the mining boom didn't pose a great enough threat to the rest of the economy to necessitate the introduction of a profits-based tax.

The task for the Gillard government is, in essence, the same task that the Rudd government could not handle when it was popular. Australia is prosperous and voters want the proceeds of the boom to be invested wisely on their behalf. The mining tax and putting a price on carbon pollution are more than just political symbols now for Labor. They will test whether the nation is capable of reform given the constraints of a hung parliament.

The 2010 election turned politics upside down by splitting the House of Representatives along state lines, while creating a historic Labor–Greens metropolitan majority in the Senate. It is not quite what the founding fathers had in mind, because the lower house was meant to be the people's chamber, while the interests of the states were to be protected in the upper house.

The result, in a nutshell, saw the mining states abandon Labor, while the southern states swung against the Coalition. New South Wales couldn't make up its mind between the main parties. Women backed Julia Gillard, men sided with Tony Abbott. The old went for the Coalition, and the young, well, this is where the game really changed. The Greens gained the support of 25 per cent of men aged 18–34 years, and almost 20 per cent of women of the same age. Julia and Tony, meet Generation Y, the voters who threaten the major-party duopoly.

I had wondered for some years what would happen to Generation Y when it faced its first recession. Born in the 1980s, this group came of age in the Howard years with a social outlook that was the antithesis of the prime minister's. Their self-absorption suggested that they would become hysterical when the easy credit ran out. Instead, the global financial crisis found them in better shape than their baby-boomer parents and their big brothers and sisters in Generation X. They behaved as the deregulation manual said they should by agreeing to reduced hours to save their jobs. When the economy improved, they figured they could either return to full-time work or swap employers.

The stress was felt further up the age scale, by Generation X and especially by the baby boomers born in the 1950s. For people aged in their fifties who are at or near retirement, the Australian economy had long seemed like a beautiful dream. These baby boomers may have suffered in the recession "we had to have," but they got the best of the recovery that followed. If they played their property cards right, they would have bought in at the bottom of the market and seen their capital gains explode over the past decade. What could they possibly have to complain about when the global financial crisis hit? Plenty. The fifty-somethings had borrowed against their capital gain to fund an increasingly indulgent life-style. Although the financial crisis didn't take away their jobs, it did end the party. Having their hours cut to save their jobs didn't appeal because the baby boomers worried they would never again return to full-time employment.

In a choice between appealing to a happy voter and appeasing a grumpy one, the standard thinking is to go to where the backlash is. But what happens when the orthodox approach offends young people because they assume, with good reason, that the nation's future belongs to them? On 21 August, Generation Y cast a pro-reform protest vote. They denied Gillard a majority for the same reason that Rudd had lost his job: inaction.

I sat in on a Generation Y focus group in the first week of the campaign. I came out thinking Gillard would win comfortably because of the things that were said about Abbott. This was before the leaks, and before the prime minister had repeated her predecessor's error of ducking the issue of climate change. My snapshot of middle Australia comprised eight women in their early to mid-twenties, living in Melbourne's southern suburbs. All were first-home buyers.

The most interesting discussion concerned spending and saving. These women have more cash now than they did as teenagers, but "there is less of it to enjoy." Their definition of thrift is to put money aside for their wedding, or to put off travelling overseas for a year. I asked why they had taken out mortgages so young. The market forced them to. If they were to wait until they were thirty, they would not be able to afford to buy. One had just moved back with her parents and was renting out her home to save money.

The sequence here is mortgage, marriage, then kids. A Coalition pollster would call these women "aspirationals."

Politics didn't come up. The researcher Rebecca Huntley, of Ipsos Mackay, prompted them by asking for thoughts on the election.

"I don't like Tony Abbott's budgie smugglers," one said.

"He creeps me out. He looks really creepy," another said.

"I saw a black and white photo of him the other day and … he looked like a criminal."

"Dodgy."

"Some of the things he says are so uneducated."

They described Gillard as thorough and composed. She was Julia to them.

"She thinks before she speaks."

They still liked Kevin Rudd, the "cool geek," even though he had gone.

"He gave us lots of money."

Asked what they did with their stimulus payments, each reply was punctuated with a giggle.

"Shopping."

"Shopping."

"Paid off the credit card and then shopped again."

"Went to Sydney."

On 21 August, the safe Labor seat of Isaacs where the focus group was held saw the Greens' primary vote climb by 4.7 per cent to 10.9 per cent. The swing was at the expense of the Liberal Party, whose primary vote slumped by 4 per cent to 34.5 per cent.

If the Liberals are on the nose in Melbourne's mortgage belt, then Labor's identity crisis could extend to the suburbs in a term or two. Counter-intuitive though this might seem, both sides understand the dynamic. Labor's trouble with the Greens begins with a collapse in the conservative vote. This brings the Greens to within reach of second place, and the opportunity to overtake Labor on preferences.

I know, I know, the two-party system has had more premature death notices than recorded music. Remember the Australian Democrats? In 1990, they secured a primary vote of 11.3 per cent in the lower house, only to see it crash to 3.8 per cent at the following election. Or Pauline Hanson's One Nation? In 1998, they were the first pick of 8.4 per cent of the electorate, but only 4.3 per cent at the next poll.

The Greens' 2010 primary vote of 11.8 per cent could easily recede to single-digits if some routine calamity drives the young back into the arms of Labor or the Coalition. But this is easier said than done while the economy remains strong. Privately, the main parties concede that the Greens represent a structural risk to their respective bases because they have so many young people already on board. If they aren't thinking Labor or Coalition in their twenties and thirties, what would make them change in middle age?

The previous outbreaks against the main parties were driven by outsiders and took place in the context of economic hardship. At its peak, One Nation attracted the support of 16 per cent of men aged fifty-plus, and 12 per cent of those aged 35–49, but their following was in single digits across all other groups. By contrast, the Greens are in double digits across all groups except men aged fifty-plus. They are a pink- and white-collar movement.

The Greens pose an institutional as well as electoral threat to Labor because they appeal to that part of the base that provides parliamentary talent: the professionals. The CV of Adam Bandt, federal member for the seat of Melbourne, mirrors Julia Gillard's. Student politics, then a career in law as a partner at Slater and Gordon. A generation ago Bandt would have joined the party of Whitlam, Hawke and Keating.

To draw a historical analogy, the urban Greens might be to the twenty-first century what the old Country Party was to the 1950s and '60s when the bush still had financial power. The Greens appeal to Generation Y in particular because the party oozes idealism. Bob Brown has become the new Kevin 07, the cheery nerd who would liberate us from the lowest-common-denominator politics of the Howard years. Now Labor knows what the Coalition felt like when Rudd first became leader.

The pollster Tony Mitchelmore says the danger for the main parties is that their core voters are just as disillusioned as those who have already taken a leap of faith to go with the Greens.

"What I'm getting in focus groups from people who didn't reach the tipping point is the same attitude, the same frustration, the same description of the behaviour they are sick of as those who have already switched to the Greens," Mitchelmore says. "Ask them to describe the typical politicians; they say they are frauds, they are not genuine, they are not authentic, they are predictably adversarial, they believe in nothing."

The acceleration in the Greens vote is being driven more by instinct than specific issues:

> It goes across a range. At one end it is almost apathy: "What have I got to lose?", "I've tried the other two, they are just going to be more of the same, so why don't I try these other guys?" At the other end of it, there is a bit of an antidote: "At least they stand for something and they have the courage of their convictions." These voters can name the environment as something that they definitely stand for. And further along the spectrum there are the voters who identify with the more left values of the Greens and are able to talk about human rights, refugees.

In her post-election analysis, Rebecca Huntley found that voters were frustrated, cynical or angry:

> They have serious problems with the two-party system – specifically the perceived lack of difference between the two major parties – and the apparent inability of our political leaders to think and act long term for the benefit of the nation. They often express their dissatisfaction with the quality of media commentary on politics as well.

There is a telling measure of disenchantment at the ballot box: the combined major-party vote. In the seventeen federal elections held between 1949 and 1987, Labor and the Coalition claimed more than 90 per cent of the first-preference votes between them in all but two of those contests. (The exceptions were 1958 and 1977, the respective debuts of the Democratic Labor Party and the Australian Democrats.)

In the eight federal elections between 1990 and 2010, only one result came close to the 90 per cent benchmark: 1993. Ring any bells? That was Australia's last genuine battle of policies and values, between Paul Keating and John Hewson.

Given that between 15 and 20 per cent of Australians have been voting none of the above for the best part of two decades, the only surprise is that it took so long to hang the parliament.

*

If only Labor and the Coalition could reconnect with their former reformist selves of the 1980s and '90s, when difficult decisions were taken, from the float of the dollar to native title, from tariff cuts to tough gun laws. If they stood for something, there'd be no need for younger voters to project onto the next cleanskin.

Sadly, there are numerous obstacles to this outcome, obvious though its virtues may be. The information revolution and the greying of the population have combined to place a handbrake on reform. As we have seen, the accelerated media cycle makes it almost impossible for leaders to persuade voters to accept decisions in the national interest if someone says no. More than half the electorate wants to impose a price on carbon pollution, but support for action is less overwhelming once pollsters start testing how much people are prepared to pay out of their own pockets. The older the voter, the greater the resistance. And herein lies the rub. Voters aged fifty-plus are fast approaching the point when they will account for half of the electorate. They were 43.9 per cent of all voters in 2007, and 46.1 per cent in 2010. Julia and Tony, meet the baby boomers, the spoilt generation that we can no longer afford to indulge.

Labor was always going to go backwards if it couldn't increase its support within the grey belt. That opportunity passed, paradoxically, with the formal escape from the global financial crisis in early 2009. Nothing the Rudd and Gillard governments offered could compensate for the destruction of retiree nest eggs. Superannuation funds had boasted double-digit returns in the final four years of the Howard government. This wasn't the Coalition's doing, any more than the subsequent falls of 8.1 per cent in 2007–08 and 11.7 per cent in 2008–09 were Labor's fault. But the financial crisis had the same effect on older people that WorkChoices had on the youth belt and working families in 2007: it made them feel poorer at a time of near-full employment.

Tony Abbott sought power on behalf of the grey belt. Stop the boats and the great big new taxes, he said. These are the empty placards of an anti-reform protest party, not the manifesto of an alternative government. But the slogans made more sense to older voters than Julia Gillard's hesitant call to move forward made to the young. Abbott played the generation gridlock card and it almost worked.

The electoral pendulum is telling the Coalition to stick to its oldies base and leave Labor to its existential crisis on the left. But this would be the right's version of power without purpose, because any party that seeks its governing mandate from those at or nearing retirement will have a vested interest in stasis.

Don't underestimate the ability of the grey belt to thwart reform in the future, and to create a generational competition that drives even more young voters away from the main parties and to the Greens.

The needs of the baby boomers collide with those of Generation Y across every conceivable policy challenge facing Australia. Restore the nation's spending on education to international standards? Not if it means baby boomers have to supply some of the spending cuts to make way for a knowledge nation. Make housing more affordable? Not if it means baby boomers lose their capital gain. Use a market-based mechanism to handle climate change? Not if it means baby boomers can't be made better off in the transition.

*

Apart from young and old, there is one other key fault-line for the nation. Travel down the east coast of Australia and Labor's vote after the distribution of preferences increased by about 5 percentage points with each crossing of the border. From 45 per cent in Queensland, to 49 per cent in New South Wales, to 55 per cent in Victoria and, over the Bass Strait, 60 per cent in Tasmania. The schism between Queensland and Victoria is echoed between the blue state of Western Australia (Labor's weakest, on 44 per cent) and the red state of South Australia (53 per cent). Mining states versus manufacturing states; conservative states versus progressive states.

In political and social terms, Victoria is Venus, Queensland is Mars. Victoria is the state the rest of Australia imagines itself to be – pro-market and pro-immigration. Queensland is the least urbanised state in the nation, and its capital, Brisbane, has the lowest proportion of overseas-born residents of the big four Australian cities. It has jumped from outpost to major state over the past two decades, but it has yet to lose its sense of otherness in its cultural argument with the rest of the nation.

Queensland has traditionally swung hard against Labor governments, leaving Paul Keating with just two seats in 1996 and Gough Whitlam only one in 1975. But it rarely goes against an incumbent when the rest of the nation isn't in a mood for retribution. The 2010 election was the first since 1984 when the Sunshine State backed the wrong side by giving a majority of seats to the Opposition.

To see the fractures more clearly, imagine the federal parliament as three zones of roughly equal size. The southern, or progressive, states of Victoria, South Australia, Tasmania and the ACT hold 55 seats. The mining, or conservative, states of Queensland, Western Australia and the Northern Territory have 47 seats. Sitting between the two is the dead state of New South Wales, with 48 seats.

In net terms, the southern states swung two seats to the left – 36 out of 55. New South Wales moved four seats to the right, but Labor still held the majority – 26 out of 48, plus the two rural independents it picked up afterward. The wipe-out occurred in the mining states, where Labor lost half its seats, leaving it with a miserable 12 out of 47.

Labor was on the nose in the north and the west because people felt worse off, notwithstanding Australia's artful dodge of the global recession. The crowding out associated with a resources boom affected every aspect of society, business and government in the mining states.

For the locals, cost of living pressures are exploding. For the new arrivals from interstate, home ownership is out of reach because of high prices and shortages. There are 56,000 more willing buyers than there are available houses and units in Queensland, while the supply gap in Western Australia is 30,000. And for Labor, years of cutting corners on infrastructure, health and education at the state level rebounded against a first-term federal government.

The unease in Queensland dates back to the introduction of Work-Choices in 2006. Voters began blaming John Howard for everything, including the water shortages that were a state responsibility. Sure, Queenslanders still had jobs. But the state was at near-full employment when it sacked the Coalition government in 2007.

"It's getting really hard to live in Queensland," was how Labor's post-election analysis put it.

The affairs of the states are fast becoming the most pressing concern of federal government. State Labor is exhausted in New South Wales, where it has held power for twenty-seven of the last thirty-four years. Labor's dismissal is expected next March. In Queensland, Labor has ruled for all but three of the last twenty-one years, and its chances of earning another term in 2012 are slim. These two states have the nation's least efficient energy markets, so their households will wear the sharpest spikes in prices under an emissions trading scheme or a carbon tax. But there is no point in Gillard agonising over this transaction, because federal Labor will lose even more votes to the Greens if it continues to prevaricate on climate change. New South Wales and Queensland also have the greatest need for new infrastructure spending. Without the revenue that flows from a mining tax, Gillard can't help to meet those demands.

Gillard has no choice, really, but to pursue reform, even if it means federal Labor suffers at the next election. The alternative is another term of do-nothing government, which, as 21 August demonstrated, isn't smart politics anyway.

The false economy of poll-driven government should be apparent to both sides by now. Labor ceases to be a viable stand-alone party if it cedes a generation of voters, and party members, to the Greens. For the Coalition, the demographic time bomb is ticking just as loudly. It has even less support among young voters than Labor and can't claim a positive mandate while it presents itself as a protest party for the grey belt alone.

Rudd, Gillard and Abbott sought power in 2010 on the same dangerous premise, that no sacrifice is required to secure our future. Government on this basis is never worth it because the promise of painless change can never be kept. The voters knew it, which is why they spared themselves the inevitable let-down by hanging the parliament.

Before the news and polling cycles accelerated, leaders assumed that the electorate understood reform was a long game. Not anymore. The digital age has shrunk the public attention span and lured government into making each thing it says *appear* to be a big idea.

While impatience remains the dominant instinct in politics, and in our wider culture, both sides will err on the side of hyperbole. The best ever, no, the worst in history.

And still they wonder why the backlash comes when delivery doesn't meet expectation. We saved you from recession. No, you set my roof on fire. Hang on, you let that dodgy installer into your house. It's a circular conversation that government can only break if it starts playing its role again by telling voters what is and isn't possible.

Australia has acquired a form of policy paralysis by over-analysis. The problem isn't the quality of the advice, because there is more of it than ever before if leaders know where to look. The system is broken because the prosperity generation of politicians has been too willing to junk good policy when the pollster says so.

If too much information can make you stupid, then we have seen it in the way our leaders have tried to be simultaneously expert, celebrity, philosopher and number-cruncher. Labor gave us know-it-alls in Mark Latham and Kevin Rudd. The Liberal Party's version was Malcolm Turnbull. If a policy adviser has managed to convince any of the above to change their mind without resorting to a poll, I'd like to dedicate this essay to them.

Julia Gillard's instincts are to under-promise and over-deliver. On the other hand, what makes Julia so much more normal than Mark, Kevin, Malcolm and Tony might be the very thing that prevents her from being a successful prime minister: she doesn't have the touch of madness that allows a leader to inspire.

Gillard says Australia gave Labor a mixed report card for its first term:

I think the electorate did give us a tick for the response to the global financial crisis. They did realise that the government action made a difference. But people were also sending us a series of concerns about implementation. I think there was well and truly a message about, on the one hand urban congestion, on the other hand border protection, and obviously it was in the political interests of the Opposition to conflate these concepts in people's minds. And I think on climate change there was a message too. They were saying to us they weren't sure of what the message was.

Gillard concedes that governments have yet to work out how to run meaningful debates in the digital age. Political parties have adapted new technologies for electioneering, and she cites Barack Obama's presidential campaign of 2008 as the benchmark. But this method doesn't translate to governing: "The conducting of conversations from government is different to campaign communications and I don't think the way of having a national conversation has changed yet."

The 24-hour news cycle traps governments into "conversations that are thin, but not deep," she says.

Something that was a blockbuster at 10 a.m. when it's announced has been tweeted about by 10.05, has been blogged about by 10.30. Then on 24-hour TV journalists have taken to interviewing journalists about what it may or may not mean and what politicians may or may not have been thinking when they announced it. And by midday someone will be ringing my press office saying, "Have you got a story for me?" That's the nature of the cycle and I think we are still adapting to that change. One of the things I'm trying to signal by saying my focus isn't going to be the six o'clock news is to try and work through how we sustain deep conversations rather than thin conversations in this environment.

She isn't saying less is more, but that saying the same thing more often, and in different ways, is what government should be aiming for:

> I think part of the lesson for government is if you are going to sustain deep conversations then you need to be very clear about your priorities and pick what you are investing in in terms of those conversations. You won't be able to have it across this huge broad range of fronts.

The logic of this observation is that Gillard will need to risk ignoring the media when she has nothing new to say, or when the citizenry's attention is distracted by, say, another round of kiss-and-tell stories about Tiger Woods.

Gillard has a radical thought about the hung parliament. She says it will re-earth politicians and the media by making both concentrate on the legislative process. It's an optimistic view that assumes the distinctiveness of minority government will prompt journalists to reconsider how they report politics.

She had already intended to change the way government operated, to give the caucus a greater say in the formulation of legislation. Gone is Rudd's gang of four, of which she was a member:

> Whether or not we'd had the hung parliament, it was my intention to have a different way of working in caucus so people are involved in the ideas-generation stage, so they can put things on the table rather than [cabinet saying], "Here's a fully formed idea, yes or no," and then the parliamentary process is, "Here's the fully formed idea, are you for it or against it?" This is going to be a different way of working for us internally, for us as a parliament, and I think in terms of sustaining national conversations that will actually help.

But there are also some disturbing aspects to the hung parliament that suggest not much will be achieved. A hung parliament contains a hint of politics the American way, where power is bought one contrary MP at a time. The independents mostly played it straight in the negotiations to form minority government, and they made the nation feel a little better about itself as it watched the main parties crawl. The New South Wales rural independents, Tony Windsor and Rob Oakeshott, and the Tasmanian independent, Andrew Wilkie, didn't go to the highest bidder, because Tony Abbott offered them much more money. But they did extract cash for their causes. Legislation on the same terms would be messy at best, and damaging to the nation at worst.

*

Logic suggests that the revival of policy-driven government should follow the exhaustion of the poll-driven alternative. For Labor, the example of Rudd and the reality of a hung parliament ought to loosen the grip of the polling and media cycles on its collective psyche. A good poll or two from now on can't be taken seriously because Rudd had them for two years before losing his job. Equally, a bad poll or two can't make the government any more vulnerable, because it has already ceded its majority.

An optimist would see Gillard's modest personal approval rating, and Labor's continued weak primary vote, as a blessing. With no lead to protect, she can only rebuild Labor's standing through achievement, one negotiated piece of legislation at a time. Yet government is not the ideal place from which to remake a political party. Labor's greatest periods of renewal came in Opposition after heavy defeats. Gough Whitlam took the Labor leadership after the 1966 election thrashing and modernised the party's social program within two terms. Bill Hayden took another two terms to restore Labor's economic credibility after the profligacy of the Whitlam government. Hayden is the often forgotten co-author of the Hawke–Keating reforms. He was the first Labor leader to embrace the market and the now outdated notion that new spending has to be paid for by cuts elsewhere or through increased taxation. Gillard needs to channel both Whitlam and Hayden if her minority government is to effect change.

Any reform that Gillard secures will no doubt have poll-watchers obsessing again as they run a line through the public response. Here's a quick guide to reading these things: the first poll is meaningless because it usually favours the decision-maker. Paul Keating received a healthy bounce in his personal rating after the *Mabo* legislation was passed in December 1993; John Howard enjoyed a similar improvement after he struck his GST deal with the Australian Democrats in May 1999. The voters pay on results, but they are liable to ask for their money back if the implementation goes awry. The harder task for any government is to keep the conversation going.

Gillard's checklist for reform begins with an issue where very few Labor seats are directly at risk: the Murray–Darling basin. Water is an issue that both sides supposedly agree on, and Labor will rely on Howard-government legislation for its proposed buy-back of irrigation licences to restore flows to the river system. The premise of water reform is that too many licences were issued by state governments in the past, compromising the very viability of the Murray–Darling. This process will be difficult because country towns that rely on irrigation will have to find new sources of income. Unlike most reforms, though, water is one area where the losers can be compensated on generous terms, at the expense of the general taxpayer. If the government purchases water on behalf of the environment, the farmers concerned receive a cash buffer that they can use either to diversify their crop or to seek work in another field. Manufacturing workers did not enjoy the same luxury when the tariff wall came down in the 1980s and '90s. They bore the cost of a reform that benefited the wider community.

The environment was Labor's home turf until it botched the emissions trading scheme. The people were prepared to pay, but Rudd and then Gillard hesitated. Yet Labor had reason to believe that sacrifice for the environment had become a popular cause because when state governments tested support for water restrictions, they found, to their surprise, that the public was happy to contribute. One Labor premier told me that he couldn't *ease* the restrictions for fear of a voter backlash.

The independents want to act as Labor's conscience, nudging Gillard and her ministers towards reforms that were deemed too hard in the first term. There seems to be a commonality of interests here because the prime minister will want to secure her base in the southern states, and recapture some of the Labor defectors who went to the Greens, by legislating for a mining tax and a price on carbon pollution.

But these are the two agendas that helped turn Queensland against Labor. The Opposition leader will be under pressure to continue to obstruct both if he wants to keep the mining states in the Coalition camp. The tightness of the numbers gives Abbott the opportunity to play the game hard, Malcolm Fraser-style. He might recall that the electorate didn't punish the conservatives for the crisis of 1975, even though it was their manipulation of the Senate casual vacancy process that allowed them to defer supply to the Whitlam government – the precondition for Labor's dismissal.

Australia's crisis of governance is part of a global pattern. Great Britain has a hung parliament, and the United States has been testing new forms of gridlock. Barack Obama has some big reforms to his name, most notably on health care, but he is cursed with the same decline in popularity as the do-nothing Rudd and Gillard governments.

The president blames himself for assuming that reform would sell itself. "Given how much stuff was coming at us, we probably spent much more time trying to get the policy right than trying to get the politics right," he told the *New York Times* in an interview published in October 2010.

> There is probably a perverse pride in my administration – and I take responsibility for this; this was blowing from the top – that we were going to do the right thing, even if short-term it was unpopular. And I think anybody who's occupied this office has to remember that success is determined by an intersection in policy and politics and that you can't be neglecting of marketing and PR and public opinion.

Damned if you reform, and damned if you don't.

Obama carries the handicap of an unemployment rate that is double ours. Yet his experience is nonetheless familiar. Obama's approval rating displayed a Rudd-like quality in the early stages. In fact, his numbers in the first 100 days of his presidency were the strongest in a generation – better than those of Ronald Reagan, the two George Bushes and Bill Clinton at the same stage. Then came the steady slide from a percentage figure in the high 60s to the low 40s. Obama's trajectory after almost two years in office is identical to that of Reagan, who also inherited an economy in deep recession.

While Australians may never entertain the extremes of the American psyche of god, guns and greed, our politicians do adopt the American habits of government and Opposition. Rudd wanted to be Obama, the messiah, and Tony Abbott has taken a leaf from the book of Sarah Palin, the snark in exile. The Opposition leader looked to the United States and saw that the Republicans could rough up a popular Democrat president who had control of both houses of congress simply by saying "No."

Obama admits that he underestimated the ability of the Republicans to slow down the legislative process at his expense. In September he told *Rolling Stone* magazine:

> Even if you eventually got something done, it would take so long and it would be so contentious, that it sent the message to the public that "Gosh, Obama said he was going to come in and change Washington, and it's exactly the same, it's more contentious than ever."
>
> Everything just seems to drag on – even what should be routine activities, like appointments, aren't happening. So it created an atmosphere in which a public that is already very sceptical of government, but was maybe feeling hopeful right after my election, felt deflated and sort of felt "We're just seeing more of the same."

The global financial crisis has been a killer of incumbents, flipping the mood that existed immediately after the 11 September 2001 terrorist attacks when almost every government around the world recorded swings to it.

The financial crisis has pitted young against old, and it has compounded the two trends that have undermined government. The long story is the end of the Cold War, which has forced the major parties to exaggerate the ideological differences that remain between them – a squabble that turns off voters. The more recent catalyst is the internet. Australia has not been immune from these forces, despite its two-decades-long boom.

Journalists fear their loss of authority in the digital age will undermine their ability to hold government to account. Yet government has much more to worry about because the internet has empowered vested interests, and Oppositions, in a way that can effectively cancel an election result within weeks of the final ballot being counted. Obama used the internet to market his genius in 2008. But his strategic insight was applied against him in office because his opponents uncovered the veto of white noise. They could yell and blame him for the ruckus, because he was the fancy-pants who had promised change. The Coalition hit on the same idea late in Rudd's first term, but the results were just as spectacular. Rudd had a meltdown, and Gillard almost went the same way.

The fact that a prosperous Australia suffers a version of the politics that cripples a recessed United States suggests the explanation is structural, not cyclical. Western democracies, I fear, are fast approaching the point where they become ungovernable because anyone can say "No."

Government is weaker today because the public it serves is quicker to anger, and because the Opposition has realised the safest way back to power is opposition, not policy renewal. No mandate need be respected because the Opposition can trust the media to set impossible standards for governments to meet.

The American polls show that what politics has lost over the past generation is respect. The last US president who appealed to both sides of politics was Reagan. Every president since then has drawn the bulk of his approval rating from his party's supporters only – the other side marked him so low you could swear they were biased. This is their version of Australia's large none-of-the-above primary vote since 1990. We share a political culture that is both polarised and disengaged.

Reagan ruled in the 1980s, when Bob Hawke and Paul Keating were at the peak of their reformist powers. The Liberals back then offered Labor bipartisanship on the two most crucial elements of the reform push: the floating of the dollar and the removal of tariff protection. The Liberals did oppose Medicare, the assets test for the age pension, the capital-gains tax and, later, universal superannuation. But they gave Labor respect where it mattered.

The emissions trading scheme should have marked a return to form for our system. On any fair reading of the numbers in the parliament, two-thirds of all MPs – that is, most on the Labor side, the Greens and up to half the Coalition – supported action on climate change. Yet minority interests prevailed. Polluters extracted concessions that made the budget worse off, before the half of the Opposition who didn't believe in climate change scuttled the compromised legislation. If Australia can't secure reform where majority support already exists, then it has taken the first step on the road back to mediocrity.

What makes me pessimistic about the nation's politics now is the char-acter of many of the people in it. The crew that delivered us such a silly campaign have to behave like adults to make the hung parliament work. They will need to overcome a generational instinct for instant gratification.

Before they can re-educate the electorate, they must first re-train themselves.

SOURCES

6 "Between 1940 and 1987, Labor recorded ...": Here are Labor's primary votes each time it took government from Opposition since World War II:

> 1972 49.6 per cent
> 1983 49.5 per cent
> 2007 43.38 per cent

And the primaries since 1990:

> 1990 39.4 per cent
> 1993 44.9 per cent
> 1996 38.8 per cent
> 1998 40.1 per cent
> 2001 37.8 per cent
> 2004 37.6 per cent
> 2007 43.38 per cent
> 2010 37.99 per cent

9 "press secretary David Luff revealed ...": David Luff, "PM needs something to numb his pain," *The Sunday Telegraph*, 1 June 2008.

12–13 "When I fought the 1997 election ...": Tony Blair's speech was given on 12 June 2007, fifteen days before he resigned as prime minister. See http://news.bbc.co.uk/2/hi/uk_news/politics/6744581.stm.

17 "Menzies and Murdoch engaged in an angry exchange ...": The account of the Menzies–Murdoch feud is sourced to Bridget Griffen-Foley's *Party Games: Australian Politicians and the Media from War to Dismissal*, Text, Melbourne, 2003, pp. 24–28. Griffen-Foley says that "there is no evidence to suggest that he [Sir Keith Murdoch] had deliberately solicited a poll to destabilise Menzies' leadership." I think a reverse burden of proof should apply in these cases: a politician should be assumed to be paranoid unless he can prove otherwise.

17 "If it serves to tell the politician ...": *New York Times Magazine*, 28 November 1948.

17 "The early polls also showed ...": Gallup poll taken on 30 March 1951.

22 "[His] first memory is of the steam train ...": Michael Duffy, *Latham and Abbott: The Lives and Rivalry of the Two Finest Politicians of Their Generation*, Random House, Milson's Point NSW, 2004, p. 10.

23 "Abbott gave a speech calling for tolerance ...": The Opposition leader gave his Big Australia speech on 22 January 2010 in Melbourne. See www.tonyabbott.com.au/latestnews/speeches/tabid/88/articletype/articleview/articleid/

7228/address-to-the-australia-day-council-victoria-australia-day-dinner-melbourne.aspx.

31   "Like two old bulls who didn't know when to stop charging …": The Hawke–Keating section is adapted from my article "Paul Keating unleashes on Bob Hawke: I carried you through years of 'malaise,'" *The Australian*, 15 July 2010.

40   "But only after saying he wouldn't compromise": John Howard made the comment on 19 February 2001.

47   "Ross Garnaut used a lecture …": "Climate Change, China Booms and Australia's Governance Struggle in a Changing World," 2010 Hamer Oration, University of Melbourne and Hamer Family Fund, 5 August 2010.

48-49 "Treasury had sharp words for both sides …": The Blue Book was released by Shadow Treasurer Joe Hockey. The incoming brief for the Labor government, the Red Book, can be found at www.treasury.gov.au/contentitem.asp?ContentID=1875&NavID=007.

51   "telling the pollsters they preferred increased spending to tax cuts …": See Juliet Clark and Ian McAllister, *Trends in Australian Political Opinion: Results from the Australian Election Study 1987–2007*, p. 29, available at http://assda.anu.edu.au/aestrends.pdf; and Richard Grant, *Less Tax or More Social Spending: Twenty Years of Opinion Polling, Information and Research Services*, Parliamentary Library, Department of Parliamentary Services, 2004, available at www.aph.gov.au/library/pubs/rp/2003-04/04rp13.pdf.

55-56 "Tom Albanese, went on Sydney talkback radio …": 2GB, 3 June 2010. Media Monitors transcript.

56   "In his book on the Chinese Community Party …": Richard McGregor, *The Party: The Secret World of China's Communist Rulers*, Harper Collins, New York, 2010, p. 61.

57   "state income during the global financial crisis …": Figures taken from the Australian Bureau of Statistics report 5220.0, *Australian National Accounts: State Accounts, 2008-09*. The 2009–10 figures are due for release on 19 November 2010. They will shed further light on Queensland's economic performance in the election year.

59   "For the first time in our history …": I've taken Brian Loughnane's speech from Malcolm Farnsworth's blog, *AustralianPolitics.com*, "Liberal Party Director Analyses Election Defeat," 19 December 2007.

62   "The result, in a nutshell …": Newspoll, unpublished demographic breakdown. I've rounded the totals, as these numbers jump around a bit from poll to poll. The 17–19 August results were:

Men aged 18–34: Labor 29.9 per cent, Coalition 36.6 per cent, Greens 25.5 per cent. Women aged 18–34: Labor 39.3 per cent, Coalition 32.9 per cent, Greens 18.1 per cent.

63   "I sat in on a Generation Y focus group …": focus group conducted as part of the *Ipsos Mackay Report*.

64   "On 21 August, the safe Labor seat …": Election results sourced from the AEC's Virtual Tally Room (http://vtr.aec.gov.au). The final count for Isaacs can be found at http://vtr.aec.gov.au/HouseDivisionFirstPrefs-15508-219.htm.

65   "At its peak, One Nation …": Newspoll, unpublished demographic breakdown for the September quarter, 1998. One Nation's total primary vote among men was 12.2 per cent, but for women it was 7.7 per cent.

66   "There is a telling measure of disenchantment at the ballot box …": Figures taken from the *AEC Electoral Pocketbook*, revised edition, April 2009.

67   "Superannuation funds had boasted double-digit returns …": Figures taken from Table 13, *Annual Superannuation Bulletin*, June 2009. Available at www.apra.gov. au/Statistics/Annual-Superannuation-Publication.cfm.

68   "one other key fault-line for the nation …": Labor's two-party vote for each state, travelling north to south and east to west, to two decimal points:

        Queensland 44.86 per cent
        New South Wales 48.84 per cent
        Victoria 55.31 per cent
        Tasmania 60.62 per cent
        South Australia 53.18 per cent
        Western Australia 43.59 per cent

70   "For the locals, cost of living pressures are exploding …": See Table 4.5 of the National Housing Supply Council's 2010 State of Supply Report, www.nhsc.org. au/state_of_supply/2009_ssr_rpt/SoSR_ch4.htm#ch4_2.

I conducted dozens of interviews before and after the 2010 election. The following are the dates of the interviews that yielded for-the-record quotes. The other politicians, party figures and officials I spoke to will, of course, remain nameless.

The politicians: John Howard, 20 September; Wayne Swan, 22 September; Simon Crean, 23 September; and Julia Gillard, 29 September.

The pollsters: Rod Cameron, founder of ANOP, 15 September; Neil Lawrence, founder of Lawrence Creative Strategy, 18 September; and Tony Mitchelmore, founder of Visibility, 21 September.

Correspondence

Gareth Evans

Hugh White has opened up an uncomfortable debate – but one that we need to have – about whether it is reasonable to assume that Australia can go on enjoying indefinitely both a hugely prosperous economic relationship with China and a hugely reassuring security relationship with the US in an environment where the tectonic plates really are shifting, and where it cannot be assumed that China will continue to recognise – as over time it becomes economically dominant – the primacy of US power.

His basic point, which may have been obscured by the subsequent static, is plausible enough. China is much more likely to seek a balance of power – or a nineteenth-century European-type "concert of powers" – in the broader Asia of the future than to try to impose a harsh hegemony backed by military force, or even the kind of "soft" hegemony imposed by the US on Latin America in the past. But China will only be able to do this if the US recognises it as a genuine equal.

White argues the US has three basic choices in responding to China's inevitable rise: to withdraw from Asia (which it is extremely unlikely to do, and allies like Australia would certainly not want it to do); to compete with China for primacy (which runs a very serious risk of ending in tears); or to be prepared seriously to share power with China (which it has so far been reluctant to do). This lays credible foundations for a serious debate, although one is left hungry for a fuller, more nuanced and, in some cases, more persuasive discussion of the premises, precise meaning and implications of each option.

There is much to contest in White's thesis, especially his description of what it would mean in practice for the US to deal with China as an equal. The way he expresses it, yielding ground in terms of advocacy, sounds more like kowtowing abdication than showing appropriate respect to a peer, or indeed to any sovereign country. My own view, after years spent conveying unpalatable truths to the great and powerful – and to many others – as foreign minister and in subsequent incarnations, is rather more robust. With a mindset of mutual respect, and with the right institutional machinery in place, there is plenty of scope for muscular bilateral and multilateral debate – and, following it, for the effective accommodation of quite different interests and worldviews.

That said, the crude vitriol that has been poured on Professor White by some commentators is wholly unjustified. He is right to open up the debate. Moreover, his description of the policy choices that will inevitably confront the major players – and Australia – seems broadly accurate; it certainly makes us think hard about how we might have to position ourselves. We cannot just assume that these hard choices will go away.

Bill Clinton (who, like several of his counterparts, seems to have got right rather more foreign-policy issues after his presidency than during it) would not have disagreed. I heard him in a discussion at Davos nearly a decade ago – when the global understanding of the scale and speed of China's rise was nothing like as acute as it is now – putting the issue of American power, its long-term limits and the policy consequences of this in a way which, to my Australian and internationalist ear, was just about pitch-perfect and deserves wider reporting than it received at the time or since:

> America has two choices. We can use our great and unprecedented military and economic power to try and stay top dog on the global block in perpetuity. Or we can seek to use that power to create a world in which we are comfortable living when we are no longer top dog on the global block.

Gareth Evans

Bruce Grant

Hugh White's valuable, if alarming, essay asserts boldly that a "Chinese challenge to American power in Asia is no longer a future possibility but a current reality." He succeeds in ruffling the feathers of both those, like myself, who thought that the US and China were accommodating each other sensibly in the post–Cold War era and those for whom any mention of a loss of American supremacy is either silly or treasonable.

The essay ends more calmly than it begins. It begins with a call to action. Power politics is back! Australia must do something! The evidence, however, is sketchy. It seems to lie in China's acquisition of new submarines and its assertion of authority in the seas around it (Yellow, East China and South China). Readers might think that China has more right than the US to police its brown waters, and whatever it may acquire in the way of a blue-water navy would be nothing compared with what the US already has. But White's argument depends on logic, not evidence. As economic wealth is the basis of military power, he argues, China's current economic strength and the United States' current economic weakness inevitably mean that American supremacy in Asia is challenged. White is a former defence official, currently an academic strategic analyst, and the essay is peppered with international-relations realist terminology – primacy, supremacy, role, contest, domination – that is not examined. He may well turn out to be right, but the case for an outbreak of contested US supremacy is not made.

When he turns to ways of "shaping the future," White adopts an insistently reasonable (if wistful) tone. A fresh and interesting idea is that "the best outcome for Australia would be for America to relinquish primacy and share power with China and the other major powers in a Concert of Asia," based on the Concert of Europe among Britain, Austria and Russia that kept relative peace in Europe for a century from the end of the Napoleonic Wars to World War I.

The difficulties, which he acknowledges, are membership (Russia?) and why China would want to submit its growing importance to the veto of a group including not just the US, but Japan and India.

White credits Henry Kissinger, with Richard Nixon, for the deal with China that brought relative peace to Asia after Vietnam. Kissinger made the Concert of Europe the centrepiece of a lifelong study of balance-of-power diplomacy. He argued that two essential conditions of its success were careful design, so that equilibrium could only be broken by a military effort of a magnitude too difficult to mount, and the fact that the warring states of Europe were nevertheless knit together by shared values.

Asia, by contrast, is an ill-defined region of baffling diversity. It contains Japan, China and ten Southeast Asian states, including Vietnam and Indonesia, as well as (in another definition) the United States, Canada and Chile, and (in another) India, Pakistan and Russia. It is not a coherent region in the way Europe is, Christian and capitalist except for Turkey, or the American hemisphere is, Christian and capitalist except for Cuba, or even Africa, divided into Christian south and Muslim north. There is no common civilisation, culture or religion: Hinduism, Buddhism, Islam, Christianity, Shintoism, Confucianism and communism are all present. Moreover, it is physically spacious and its components are separated by stretches of sea. It operates through networks, not institutions, and the energy of these networks comes from small and middle-sized countries as well as powerful states. The spirit of the region is pragmatic, looking for accommodation, consensus and compromise in the pursuit of better living conditions rather than sustaining values.

White examines other options for Australia: remain allied to the US, seek another great and powerful friend (like China, India or Japan), opt for armed (or unarmed, like New Zealand) neutrality, build a regional alliance with Southeast Asian neighbours (especially Indonesia), do nothing and hope for the best. He is critical of all five, but in the course of the survey he grapples with Australia as a "middle power," a concept he likes but is not convinced Australia has enough military muscle to fulfil.

We get a glimpse here of perhaps why White wrote this essay. He is exasperated with incompetence and inadequacy in Australia's defence. We are not spending enough (2 per cent of GDP, which will need to rise at least to 3 per cent), we are spending on the wrong things and we are not prepared to face up to what it costs to be "self-reliant" or "independent." Introspection like this has been going on since the British decided to withdraw "east of Suez" and throw in their lot with Europe. Armed, even unarmed, neutrality had a brief following on the left in Australia, as did a nuclear-armed Australia on the right. White looks back to the great debate of that period with nostalgia, arguing that another is due. Alas, coherent and articulate we may have been, but influential we were not. The nation settled for "forward defence," which got us into Vietnam and was based on the facile belief that, as we could not support forward positions on our own, the Americans would do it for us. And the "War on Terror" proved fatally attractive. Afghanistan, which could have been a short, punitive expedition, like China's incursion into Vietnam in 1979, became a long war, and Iraq proved to be what it always was, a foolhardy war of choice.

When I was writing *Australia's Foreign Relations* with Gareth Evans twenty years ago, we thought that the changes in Australia's defence outlook, resulting from Paul Dibb's report in 1986 and the Beazley White Paper that followed a year later, had, short of full-scale war, "liberated" Australia as a middle power. Whether or not we were right, a burst of activity followed. On the United Nations peace settlement in Cambodia, Australia worked first with Indonesia, then all five permanent members of the Security Council, Vietnam and the factions within Cambodia. We were instrumental in the foundation of the Asia Pacific Economic Cooperation (APEC) and the ASEAN Regional Forum (ARF) and active in the Comprehensive Nuclear-Test-Ban Treaty Organization. The Howard government later preferred bilateral diplomacy; even so, it helped to get the vote for the International Criminal Court against the opposition of the United States. Our military compatibility showed in Cambodia, where we led the UN military contingent, and in East Timor, where we led several coalitions of interested countries.

Although this activity was primarily regional, it was becoming obvious that, with the end of the Cold War, politics was global. A global system was emerging, embryonic yet increasingly tangible and fungible, compromising the self-help system that had been realism's arena for four centuries. Parts of the global system had been there for half a century or longer, including the United Nations and its agencies and the World Bank and its offspring, but they were held in check during the Cold War. New bodies, like the World Trade Organization, and hundreds, indeed thousands, of inter-government and non-government organisations were now active globally.

The world is searching for an effective forum to deal with multiple crises – financial regulation, climate change, poverty, terrorism and nuclear proliferation, to mention a few. The overriding concern is that the beggar-my-neighbour policies that led to rearmament and war in the twentieth century are not repeated. The United Nations is still a valuable forum, but it needs reform and a new generation of leaders. When it comes to action, the states themselves control the two staples of power – money and guns.

For some time, the G20 has looked the most likely candidate for international action. Kevin Rudd was one of the first as prime minter to see the benefits of this for Australia, and his "meeting of minds" with Barack Obama on the usefulness of the G20 held out hope of a new kind of alliance between Australia and the United States. There is no mention of the G20 in this essay. It is an economic grouping and Hugh White's world is the world of the nation-state, with the United Nations as a vague kind of moral and legal check on warlike tendencies in the world's 200 or so states. But these are the world's top twenty economies, and if economic strength is the basis of power, then this is the top table of global power, and for the first time in our history Australia has a seat at it.

The G8 (Britain, Canada, France, Germany, Italy, Japan, Russia and the United States) was the big-end of world politics from 1975 but, based entirely in the northern hemisphere and comprising only advanced industrial countries, it had a problem of legitimacy when speaking for the rest of the world. During the recent financial crisis, some of its members were a prime source of infection. The G20 brings together developed and developing states, adding to the G8 group Argentina, Australia, China, Brazil, India, Indonesia, Mexico, Saudi Arabia, South Africa, South Korea and Turkey. It has scope and legitimacy, representing 60 per cent of the world's population and 80 per cent of global GDP. While huge United Nations global gatherings on climate change like Kyoto and Copenhagen are unwieldy and fractious, the G20 is capable of consensus. It could even be a useful forum for the US to put pressure on China to liberalise its currency.

Having absorbed Hugh White's analysis of prospective power conflict in Australia's region, I am still inclined to look to an active Australian role in the multilateral world of the G20 rather than an assertion of traditional power through stronger defence as the way to go.

In the contemporary world, middle-power diplomacy for Australia would be typically applied to a range of problems that were not regional, but global. It would be interested in the application of rules rather than power, as interlocutor between strong states with resolute interests and those that are weak, incapacitated by internal strife or without the resources to devote to global diplomacy. It would support international law and the free exchange of ideas, people and goods. Middle powers are cooperative rather than combative, intuitive rather than assertive, and they need to be imaginative. Great powers are reluctant to be imaginative. To do so would suggest that they do not value enough their prime possession, which is power and the authority that comes with it.

Whether Australia has the diplomatic capacity for such a role is an open question. It would require resources, professional talent and intellectual persistence. It would not mean breaking the alliance with the United States, but it might test, even strain, relations from time to time, so it would need to be backed by political will. At some point, the Australian people will have to decide what kind of future they want.

Bruce Grant

Michael Wesley

With *Power Shift*, Hugh White has done two important things. In the midst of arguably the most trivial and self-obsessed period of our national life, he has reminded Australians that there are issues crucial to our long-term future that need to be discussed. And he has staked out the big question that confronts our security and prosperity over the next decades: where will the major transitions of power and wealth that are going on around us leave this country?

White uses the angular reasoning and austere language of Realpolitik to argue that a Greek tragedy is playing out to our north. China is rising inexorably. With its wealth comes a desire for influence and a capacity to do something about it. The big obstacle is America; confronted with Chinese demands for elbow room, it will either push back or pack up and go home. Rather than live with these extremes, it's in Australia's interest to convince both to share leadership in this region.

This is strategic thinking on its grandest scale: a forced focus decades into the future and a disciplined consideration of what we should be doing now to be best positioned for that future. The hardest thing about all this is looking at present trends and trying to predict how they will interact to shape the future.

White is right to focus on the rise of China; this is the single most important strategic shift that will occur in the first half of this century. But it's not the only one. The story of Asia's power shift is not just a China–America story. And if we factor in the rest of the story we get to a very different future, and a different set of strategic choices, than those posed in *Power Shift*.

Without question, China is rising faster than any other major country on the planet. It is already the centre of economic dynamism on the Asian continent, a significant force in global finance and an increasingly potent military power. This, of course, makes it a country of intense focus and concern to the United States, which has been all of these things for generations.

But China's rise hasn't occurred in isolation. It is surrounded by other considerable countries with already large (Japan) or rapidly growing (India, Vietnam) economies. Nearly all of China's neighbours have either fought against it or had seriously tense relations with Beijing in living memory. And nearly all of those neighbours are increasingly integrated with China economically.

And so China's rise has kicked off a complex dynamic among its neighbours. Desperate to avoid their economic interdependence with China turning into all-round dependence, China's neighbours are building their economies and military power as quickly as they can. They are searching for and building diplomatic and military links that offset their integration with China's economy. The last thing anyone wants is to be left alone to Beijing's tender mercies.

To be sure, China is bigger and stronger than any one of its neighbours. But even if it continues to grow at current rates, it will not become stronger than all of them. All around its long land and sea borders, China is surrounded by significant countries that don't trust it: Russia, Japan, South Korea, Taiwan, Vietnam, India. So as China has risen, particularly in recent years, we've seen relationships tighten between America and its allies in the Pacific; new friendships form between Washington and former antagonists such as India and Vietnam; and most importantly, the tendrils of mutual assistance, investment and strategic cooperation among China's neighbours: Japan–India; India–Vietnam; Korea–Indonesia. These aren't formal alliances because they don't want to provoke Beijing's paranoia, but they grow more strategically significant with each passing year.

Beijing is therefore caught in the foreign-affairs equivalent of the tar-baby story. Whenever it tries to muscle up and assert its interests against America or one of its neighbours, it scares the rest, tightens their solidarity with each other and deepens its own strategic isolation. It makes China's neighbours even more determined to preserve American power and leadership in the region.

This situation means that a central dynamic in White's Greek tragedy – a direct Chinese challenge to American primacy in the Pacific – is very unlikely to occur. With neighbours like these, Beijing simply won't have the elbow room to challenge Washington directly. China's abiding fear is strategic isolation and encirclement by a hostile coalition of countries. If it takes on the United States, or anyone else in the neighbourhood, it will make this fear more manifest.

Australia is already becoming a part of this emerging dynamic. Not that anyone's noticed, but our defence links with Japan and Korea have thickened substantially in the past couple of years. If we can get our act together, the same process could occur with India, Vietnam and Indonesia. As these dynamics play out, it would look decidedly anomalous for us to try to convince the United States to concede strategic space to China in the Pacific – because our position would be not only out of whack with our own strategic interests, but with those of most of our northern neighbours too.

This is the sort of discussion and debate we should have started years ago. Hugh White has done this country a great service in provoking it now. It's up to the rest of us to make sure we don't let it slip back into obscurity again, displaced by great matters of consequence, such as who's going to be deputy speaker.

Michael Wesley

Lyric Hughes Hale

I have been concerned for some time that Australia has become too complacent about Chinese growth, too reliant on the pleasant narrative of an unlimited upside to China's economy and its demand for commodities. It is critical to ask the question, "What is Australia's Plan B?" I have never had a satisfactory response until reading Hugh White's essay. I don't agree with all of his conclusions, but I do think that he raises issues that must be vigorously discussed and honestly examined if Australia's current prosperity is to continue apace.

China does appear to be a juggernaut, supported by the contention that it will be the richest country in the world in the next quarter-century. As all students of Chinese history know, China has never progressed along a straight line, and indeed one could make the case that China has experienced the greatest sustained turbulence over the longest period of time of any social institution on earth. China's sheer size and diversity have made this so, but current demands on key resources such as water, to name the most urgent, have created a lumbering giant that looks formidable from the outside, but which is highly stressed internally. Cracks visible to the outside world have begun to appear in the form of ten-day traffic jams, increasing autocratic control over the internet, and the awarding of the Nobel Peace Prize, revered in China, to Liu Xiaobo, a leading dissident.

Until recently in the modern period China has been internally focused, the victim of aggression rather than its perpetrator. Its mantra continues to be sovereignty, whose expression is concern about international interests with domestic consequences. Periodically isolationist, China has been, in Robert Elegant's poetic phrase, a country without diplomats. In the past few years China has been a valuable behind-the-scenes negotiator when flashpoints have occurred. But on the whole China prefers chequebook diplomacy, reasonably finding it cheaper than military intervention. Unlike the United States, China does not have as a policy goal the global export of its political system or its values. It is primarily a trading power, concerned with maintaining internal growth, without treasure to waste on ideological issues outside its borders. So the question becomes, what are the necessary conditions for China to become dominant in Asian affairs? What is missing from many discussions of the dynamics of Asian power?

The elephant in the room of this discussion is Japan. Japan is already a rich country, truly wealthy on a per-capita basis. Its alliance with the United States ensures trilateral balance in the Pacific for decades to come, especially as Japan begins the careful dance of asserting and projecting itself vis-à-vis the United States. The danger that Japan and China could band together to weaken American influence in the region is for historical reasons the most unlikely of scenarios imaginable.

That said, China does crave international recognition, which could both temper its actions and cause it to bluster as well. China and, as White says, Australia are invested in the continuation of the status quo. The balance of power might shift, but my sense is that it will not force a course correction in Australian foreign policy. To depart, perhaps, from the paradigm created by Paul Keating, Australia both is and isn't part of Asia. It has the strongest of alliances with the United States. It is extremely hard, for the Chinese as well, to see how that might change in our lifetimes.

White does a superlative job of explaining the evolution of peace in Asia over the past forty years, describing (with tongue in cheek?) a "vicious cycle of stability and peace." The likeliest disturber of this peace is North Korea. If China seeks to dominate, it would then follow that China and the rest of the world might find themselves on opposite sides of a conflict between the two Koreas. But China is a reluctant protector of the North Korean regime. The country owes billions of dollars to China, and its social policies have created unwanted immigration on the Chinese border. China cannot control North Korea, any more than the US can control Taiwan. It just appears to be so.

Twin points that White makes are highly sensible. In 1910, Norman Angell argued in *The Great Illusion* that integration of trade between nations is no barrier to war, and World Wars I and II both proved him right. White also counters the received wisdom that the current integration of the Asian economies and North America will prevent conflict. In fact, as we know, trade policy between nations can create conflict. His second observation that post-Cold War peace in Asia was the product of courageous leadership (Richard Nixon and Deng Xiaoping being prime exemplars) is extremely relevant. Do we have this kind of leadership today? No – and this nicely underlines White's point about the singularity of the past few decades of Asian history. The current vacuum in Japanese leadership, and its lack of ability to create a sustainable political framework, is one of Asia's most frightening developments. Also worrisome is growing evidence that the Japanese polity is increasingly unwilling to sacrifice national preferences to the American alliance. Prime Minister Yukio Hatoyama was toppled when he appeared to cave in to American demands over Okinawa. It could be that Japan's rise, rather than China's, disturbs the equilibrium.

However, if the status quo is destroyed in Asia, from a security point of view it really doesn't matter to Australia. Australia is and will be courted by both Beijing and Washington. As long as resources are critical to growth, Australia will continue to prosper. The danger I see is that if China stumbles, and the US is unable to rebound, the building blocks of growth that Australia exports will be less in demand. My conclusion is that the greatest threat to Australia is the global economy writ large, rather than a shift of political power within Asia. Maintaining the current balance might make for a more comfortable environment, but Australia will adapt and in fact is adapting incredibly well to the new economic realities of the region.

China's economy and wealth is still export-driven, dependent upon demand outside its borders. It is a poor country on a per-capita basis. White posits that "China's political and strategic weight will depend on its overall, rather than its per-capita, GDP." However, the gap between rich and poor, which was non-existent just thirty years ago, has risen to the level of non-socialist countries, and this will create a drag on China's wealth, power and productivity. The outmoded political features of a command economy have endured. Overlaid with the ability of the internet to transmit negative information, wage and housing inflation, corruption, the lack of effective institution-building and a nascent return of out-sourced manufacturing to the United States, China's success is not a foregone conclusion. White's premise that China will continue to rise is central to his argument for rebalancing. Conversely, the US economy could reverse its course as pent-up demand for housing finds its moment. America's ability to recover should not be discounted.

The real risk to political stability in Asia is the United States. As our misadventures in the Middle East disclose, we can invest huge amounts of blood and treasure based upon ideological interests and, dangerously, a real paucity of information. Australia, as a country without any impetus to project power, and as a resident of the region, has advantages beyond its commodities. The level of knowledge and expertise on Asia is an invisible but real resource. Perhaps Australia's role is to inform US policy and shape the regional dialogue so that unreasonable reactions to future conditions do not escalate. Australia is not a helpless observer, not a bystander, but an actor that can help to shape the future of Asia, assuring the continuation of its enviable prosperity. Hugh White's provocative essay is an example of the thought leadership that Australia can offer.

Lyric Hughes Hale

Robert D. Kaplan

Hugh White's essay is lucid and path-breaking. Let me attempt to further com-
plexify his thoughts. Because China's ascent will be tempered by the military
rise of India, and ongoing military modernisations in Japan and South Korea, as
well as by a United States whose navy and air force are declining in only the
most exceedingly gradual manner, China will not be a hegemon in Asia to the
extent that the US still is in the western hemisphere. Moreover, China will be
checked somewhat by Russia on land: the history of border tensions in the
Russian Far East means that China and Russia will probably not ultimately be able
to trust each other – any alliance between them will be tactical, not strategic.
The result of these factors: we may be going back to the era of the medieval
Islamic and Hindu trading networks in the Indian Ocean and Western Pacific
that preceded Vasco da Gama – a world in which there was a high degree of
interconnectivity around the entire southern rimland of Eurasia from the Horn
of Africa to the Sea of Japan, without any one power predominating. But in this
post-da Gama epoch, China will be first among equals – rather than the US –
because of its geography: China is indigenous to the region as America is not,
and therefore will not face the tyranny of distance to the same extent.

The current Chinese state includes the territory of a number of old Chinese
empires at their apex, even as the Chinese feel deeply the territorial intrusions
against them by outside powers in the nineteenth and twentieth centuries. This
history makes Chinese leaders particularly sensitive about sovereignty, and thus
helps explain their refined degree of territoriality in regards to the South China
Sea. The Chinese now approach the South China Sea in the way that Americans
used to approach the Caribbean in the days when it was contested. In the
nineteenth and especially the early twentieth century, during the building of the
Panama Canal, the American position was to dominate the Caribbean, even as it
was an international waterway. Americans themselves may not realise it

anymore, but, as the mid-twentieth-century Yale strategist Nicholas Spykman observed, it was the Americans' domination of the Greater Caribbean that allowed them to control the western hemisphere, and thus to affect the balance of power in the eastern hemisphere. The South China Sea is China's Caribbean. This attitude will bring China into conflict with the US and a number of Asian nations – conflict that will have to be managed for the good of all concerned.

Again, keep in mind that the end of the American age in military terms in the Western Pacific and the Indian Ocean has been, and probably will be, gradual. The troop draw-down in Iraq and the plateau in troop numbers in Afghanistan – with withdrawals likely in coming years – may well allow the US to focus more on East Asia. The appointment of special presidential envoys to Israel–Palestine and Afghanistan–Pakistan has freed up the secretary of state's time to focus more on competing with China – although you will never get anyone in the State Department to admit this. A useful analogy may be Great Britain. The British Royal Navy began to decline in the 1890s, but that did not stop Britain from helping to win two world wars very far into the twentieth century. Thus, while the American decline in East Asia has already begun, America could remain a pivotal regional power for quite a few decades.

Robert D. Kaplan

Harry Gelber

The final sentence in Hugh White's essay reads: "For Australia, foreign affairs and defence policy are getting serious again." Yet one of the most – possibly the most – significant aspect of the August 2010 federal election campaign was that neither Labor nor the Liberals, nor the Greens nor the "independents," seemed to have a single word to say about any concerns beyond the shores of the Australian continent. Is there a disconnect here?

But notions of inevitable "power shifts," let alone of necessary Sino–American dispute, are questionable. China has had a central place in the American view of the world since the nineteenth century. It had a key role in US planning during the Pacific war against Japan. It was at US insistence that China became one of the "Big Five" on the Security Council of the brand-new United Nations. For President Dwight D. Eisenhower in the 1950s and all his successors, a key lesson of the Korean War was that never again must America find itself fighting a land war against China in Asia. President Nixon brought Mao Zedong the priceless gift of his visit to Beijing – redolent as it must have been for every Chinese of the long centuries when foreign potentates brought tribute to the feet of the emperor. In the Vietnam War, the real winner was China. Not because of the guns and gunners it supplied to Ho Chi Minh, or even because of Beijing's role in helping to manage the eventual settlement, but because Washington's determination never to push China into intervention allowed North Vietnam to become a secure base for its own campaign in the south, creating for the Americans a strategic handicap they could never overcome. Furthermore, ever since Eisenhower, and reinforced by the "Nixon doctrine" of 1969, everyone has known that the US default posture in Asia has been offshore, with the option of supplementary onshore diplomatic, economic or military activities if or when desirable. There has been no sign of a US willingness to abandon that stance.

So it is not in the least surprising that the decades since Mao's death have seen a steadily growing, albeit incomplete and in some ways fragile, measure of Sino–American interdependence. China's dramatic economic growth has been substantially fuelled by access for its manufactures to US markets. China has used its dollar earnings for substantial investments in the US, not least in very large holdings of US treasury bonds. These things cannot be liquidated easily or quickly without damage to China itself, including the very US markets on which China's exports rely. Although China is slowly diversifying its holdings, the US dollar remains the world's leading trading and exchange currency. And since China's banks are closely controlled by the Communist Party, not everyone else will want to invest heavily in the renminbi. The central if unofficial grouping now trying to manage global monetary affairs consists of the reserve bank governors of the US, the euro, the UK, Japan and China, with the US calling most of the shots.

Nor is it an accident that many of the bright young men ("the princelings") who are especially prominent in China's banking and finance sector – including the sons of President Hu and Prime Minister Wen Jiabao – have North American finance and business degrees. Similar points might be made about technology and medical and other scientific research. And that is not even to mention the impact of American "soft power" in China, in the form of music, films, fashions and so on.

It was always inevitable, and certainly widely expected, that as China's population and resources grew, so too would its desire to reassert its traditional primacy in its own region, and its wish to become one of the world's great powers. All the signs have been that everyone in Europe and America is more than willing to accept these wishes even before China's economic, military and political resources necessarily justify them. They are also in line with the basic bargain that, since the fading of Maoism, the impenetrable and all-powerful governing Communist Party has made with the people of China. It is two-fold. First, we will gradually but steadily restore China's unity and greatness. Second, you can make as much money as you like, but don't interfere in politics.

In enforcing these rules, albeit with care, China's leaders have proved ruthlessly unsentimental. No economic, religious or social group is allowed to exist without party supervision and control, least of all any group that might conceivably become the focus for alternative politics. That does not, of course, mean that the party disregards public opinion. On the contrary, its leaders are acutely aware of the historical precedents of peasant rebellions, or the way in which the Gorbachev reforms in the former USSR got out of hand. They are therefore much concerned with public protests, for instance about intra-party corruption.

There are tens, even hundreds of thousands, of such popular protests each year, mostly against local land seizures and corrupt officials. And there is much concern about the huge differences in wealth and lifestyle between the great cities and the back-country.

To be sure, such discontent might spread. But communist rule also has some remarkable echoes of the imperial past. New incoming dynasties were often led by an overwhelmingly dominant figure, only to be succeeded by leaders of steadily declining capacity and authority. In 1989 Mao's immediate successor, Deng Xiaoping, still had the personal authority over the party and the PLA to order the army to shoot at people in Tiananmen Square. It is much less clear that the PLA would obey Hu Jintao in the same way in 2010 or 2011.

The party has other difficulties. China has very serious environmental problems, including air pollution, fouled rivers and shortages of water. (During the 2008 Olympics water had to be diverted from surrounding towns and villages to ensure that there was plenty for the hotels and fountains of Beijing to impress foreigners.)

And there is demography: labour shortages are already leading to claims for wage increases. And the population is ageing: in coming years fewer working people will have to look after the aged in a country virtually without social services. There are educational and industrial and technological problems too. No one denies that China has people of remarkable brilliance in many fields. But brilliance is not enough if the industrial and technological back-up is weak. Stealing industrial and other secrets from Germany or the US is fairly easy, but how quickly can the knowledge be used in Chinese practice?

Then there is the promise about restoring the unity and greatness of China. Unity now means absorbing every square metre of land and people that China may ever in its history have ruled or claimed: not just Tibet, Xinjiang and Taiwan but sea areas off the coast, including the South China Sea, and claims along India's Himalayan border. China is not a nation in the Western sense; it is, and always has been, an empire. As Tibet and Xinjiang have shown in recent times, not everyone accepts Chinese rule quietly. And while none of China's neighbours will seek a quarrel with Beijing, it is also a fact that none of them is an ally, except maybe North Korea and Burma. The rest of Asia – in its saner moments, maybe even Iran? – seems quite content to have the Americans around.

Hugh White is right to want people to think, not just about the quotidian present but about scenarios for the future. With his long experience as a senior official in Defence and Intelligence, he knows all about the difficulties of making governments think about even the more unlikely possibilities. Although one should not pay too much attention to overheated rhetoric, whether from Chinese admirals or US senators, the unexpected can always happen, and quite often does.

But it is difficult to accept some of his basic concepts. "Asia" is merely an abstraction. The reality is separate sovereign states with widely divergent interests. Then there is "Chinese power." But "power" too is an abstraction. China's power when dealing with Burma is not the same as China's power when discussing with Indonesia their respective claims in the South China Sea. Power varies greatly in time, place, occasion and the nature and determination of the interlocutor. Nor can power be simply assessed in terms of aggregate gross domestic product numbers, even if, in this case, Chinese statistics were more reliable than they notoriously are. The relevance of population numbers also varies hugely with education levels and industrial and technological back-up, not to mention national infrastructure.

White is, of course, right to stress that China will continue to grow and that its economic and industrial shadow will lengthen too. China will also want more control of its coastal waters and more influence in nearby sea regions. But how could China deprive the US of a serious presence in the Western Pacific, even if it wanted to? The US has shown no sign of any willingness to abandon or downplay the Japanese alliance, or assets like the US forces stationed in Okinawa or South Korea, or bases like Guam.

It is true that China's fleet visits to the Gulf and its participation in antipirate operations off the Horn of Africa will give its sailors and commanders useful experience and show China's flag there for the first time in 600 years. It seems certain that China's missile and naval forces will become larger and more powerful, perhaps acquiring the capacity to attack, even sink, a hostile carrier or disrupt an enemy's electronics. But growing a whole state-of-the-art navy is a slow business and the US, Japan and even Russia will not stand still while such things are developed. In the meantime, although China has quite a number of submarines, not all of them are very modern. Any Chinese admiral worth his salt might hesitate to expose them in serious operations against American (or Japanese?) attack boats.

In any event, it seems quite possible that "cyber war" will prove to be, in its own way, as much of a game-changer in warfare as the appearance of ironclad battleships was in the late nineteenth century, when they shocked the Royal Navy into realising that almost its entire fleet was obsolete. But here, too, would one really back the clever Chinese whiz-kids against the US research and communications groups, in both hardware and software, that range from Boston to Houston to Silicon Valley and from Microsoft to Apple and many others, not to mention the bright teenagers working for the National Security Agency and its sister organisations?

One other consideration is worth mentioning. Although Hugh White is right to concentrate on the importance of the Western Pacific, there is more to be said. For example, China has made itself heavily dependent on oil and, now, on food from the Middle East and Africa. Hence China's development of ports and other facilities in Burma, Bangladesh, Sri Lanka and Pakistan and talk of rail and pipe-line links from some of these into China. These developments will alarm India, which regards the Indian Ocean as its own bailiwick, and may raise questions about the long-term security of the Strait of Malacca. America will certainly try to maintain its westabout, trans-Indian Ocean access to Diego Garcia and the Middle East. Washington would surely react if that seemed likely to be affected by Sino–Indian or other tensions. At the same time, Australia cannot avoid creating some port and defence facilities in west and northwest Australia to pro-tect its increasingly important resource and energy operations and exports to China from there. It would be surprising if the US did not have an interest in such facilities and their potential use for a US presence in the Indian Ocean.

Perhaps closer Australian relations with Southeast Asia and an inoffensive grouping of the US, Japan and Australia (and even New Zealand?) will go on making a lot of sense for quite a while yet; perhaps more so than some of Hugh White's other scenarios.

Harry Gelber

David Uren

Hugh White sees the rise of Chinese military influence in the region as a simple function of the increasing size of its economy and wealth of its people. With wealth comes a desire for status which, in national terms, is expressed militarily. "It seems very unlikely that, as China's economy grows to match America's, its people will still willingly accept a subordinate position to America ... The richer they become, the more impatient they will be for their leaders to assert a bigger role for China in Asia," he writes. On the ABC's *Lateline*, White expressly rejected the idea that China's exercise of military power might have anything to do with narrow economic interest: "The big strategic competitions in history don't take place over economically rational things like access to resources."

However, economic interest has often been at the heart of international conflict – an obvious example is Japan's 1940s attack on Southeast Asia to gain access to its oil and rubber in the face of US and British embargoes. German expansionism in the 1930s was the result of the crushing economic burden imposed by the Versailles treaty. More recently, Ronald Reagan's military build-up in the Middle East in the early 1980s was designed to secure oil supplies in the wake of the failure of the post-OPEC strategy of energy self-sufficiency pursued by presidents Nixon and Ford.

Understanding the interplay of economic relationships sheds light on both China's military expansion and the strategic choices facing Australia and the United States. China's naval expansion – for which the Chinese slogan is "far seas defence" – is explicitly about protecting its commercial sea lanes. There was hoopla in March when two Chinese warships docked in Abu Dhabi, the first time its navy had visited the Middle East. "With the expansion of the country's economic interests, the navy wants to better protect the country's transportation routes and the safety of our major sea lanes," Rear Admiral Zhang Huachen, the deputy commander of the East Sea Fleet, told Xinhua news agency.

The former treasurer Peter Costello and his department were remarkably far-sighted when, in 2006, they made use of Australia's chairmanship of the G20 to put energy and resource security on the agenda. It was a time of rising oil prices and global concern about energy supplies. Costello's goal was to use the G20 forum to persuade the Chinese that their best guarantee of energy security was well-functioning markets.

China's instincts have been to pursue resource nationalism, with direct ownership and control of its supplies, building its own resource provinces in the old colonial stamping grounds of Africa. The major Arab oil suppliers have nationalised their oil fields and do not permit foreign investment from anyone. Hence the Chinese have built oil supplies in nations where they can make equity investments, such as the war-torn Sudan and Congo.

Costello argued that attempts by G20 nations to "lock in" supplies would precipitate a global competition for control of resources which would in fact destabilise security of supply and raise the potential for conflict. Free and transparent markets, in the end, deliver goods where they are most needed at the fairest possible price. His deputy Treasury secretary, Martin Parkinson, quoted Keynes: "If the distribution of the European coal supplies is to be a scramble in which France is satisfied first, Italy next, and everyone else takes their chance, the industrial future of Europe is black and the prospects of revolution very good."

In November 2006, as demonstrators hurled rocks at police outside Melbourne's Hyatt Hotel, the debate on resource security inside at the G20 finance ministers' meeting did not go entirely to plan. Although the communiqué reflected Australia's position, China apparently interpreted remarks that the high price of oil was a simple consequence of rising demand in a free market as a national criticism. "There are some international calls to blame China for the current global price hike in oil and other resources," the finance minister, Jin Renqing, told Chinese television at the conclusion of the meeting. "That blame is groundless and not true. China depends on its own resources and our development policy is one of energy self-reliance."

One of the first issues Kevin Rudd had to deal with as prime minister was Chinalco's proposed investment in Rio Tinto. He was decisive, with the government putting out new foreign-investment guidelines for state-owned enterprises to ensure that there were strict and plainly understood controls on Chinese ownership of Australian natural resources. Over major resource assets, Chinese investors were to be kept at arm's length. Rudd's insight that the Chinese would not accept free and transparent markets as a sufficient guarantee of their resource security was partly self-fulfilling. By putting up barriers to Chinese investment,

Australia communicated to China that it was not in fact accepted as a free-market participant.

Although it was not stated publicly, Rudd's concern was linked to China's development of a blue-water navy. Rudd saw a long-term strategic threat to Australia in China's desire to secure its supply of resources through ownership and control. Rudd's Defence White Paper identified the protection of northwest Australia as a key challenge. "Many of our key resource-extraction facilities are remote and would be vulnerable to interference, disruption or attack." The paper's biggest call – the funding of twelve new submarines – was mainly about defending the sea lanes. The paper did not mention any specific threat to those facilities, but the fact that it is possible to think about China in this regard highlights the gulf between our strategic relationships with China and the United States.

These are early days in China's emergence as a superpower. The relationship between Australia and China remains sound, with the tussle over Rio Tinto blamed by at least some Chinese authorities on their own inexperience in the ways of the capitalist world. But these are the underlying issues that will shape Australia's strategic relationship with China and the choices we make about our alliances.

The strategic rivalry of the United States and China cannot be separated from the asymmetry in their economic relationship, with the US dependent on the Chinese to finance its budget deficit. US debts to China now approximate US$1 trillion. The weight of America's financial obligation to China is radically different from its Cold War rivalry with the Soviet Union. It has become lore that the collapse of the Soviet Union was precipitated by its inability to match Reagan's overwhelming financial commitment to his "Star Wars" nuclear defence.

Much like Britain in the wake of World War II, the United States may eventually find it difficult to finance the global reach of its military. As things stand, Chinese support for the US budget deficit helped finance the wars in Iraq and Afghanistan, a point President Obama has obliquely acknowledged.

In the indefinite time-frame that White is talking about, it is possible these financial imbalances will be resolved. A surge of American productivity, a strong global recovery and the awakening of a Chinese consumer economy may transform what now seem intractable problems into historical hiccups. It was only ten years ago that the United States last reported a budget surplus. But right now, this does not seem likely. At some stage the US will have to confront politically daunting cutbacks in government services alongside hefty tax increases.

The alternative is default, achieved either by stealth, allowing inflation to erode the value of obligations to Chinese creditors or, as the Tea Party group on the right of the Republican Party advocates, outright repudiation. There is already an unhealthy tension creeping into economic relations between the two super-powers.

International conflict has many sources, including the simple jostling of national egos that White puts at the heart of his essay. However, one does not have to take a determinist view about the power of money to see that economic interests play a vital role in framing the uncomfortable strategic choices ahead.

David Uren

Hugh White

Identity is such an edgy thing for all of us – groups as much as individuals – and in national life there is nothing edgier than national identity. Inevitably, national identity plays a big part in the way we approach international relations: how we see ourselves and how we relate to others are two sides of the same coin. So any discussion of the foundations of our foreign policy is going to touch sensitive nerves, and any suggestion that those foundations might need to be realigned, or even overturned, is going to meet visceral opposition.

But such discussions must sometimes take place, because the domestic and international circumstances within which foreign policy functions do sometimes change profoundly. When that happens our policies have to change too, or they will stop working. Effective foreign policy matters to us – as a country and as individuals. In Australia we find that easy to forget because for many decades our region has mostly been so peaceful and prosperous. We slip into thinking that foreign policy is about expressing and projecting our self-image and identity to others. We need to be reminded that it is about much more elemental things and that we cannot take security and prosperity for granted. Sometimes we need to find the resilience and confidence to adapt and reinvent ourselves if we are to preserve these things.

My essay raises deep questions about Australia's place in the world, and it does so in rather stark terms. That starkness is deliberate. It seems the best way to present the issues as clearly and accurately as possible, and it also has the advantage of setting out honestly, without evasion or obfuscation, the uncomfortable choices we have to face about our place in the world as Asia changes over the next few decades. That means the essay touches none too gently on sensitive points which some people would rather leave undisturbed. As I wrote it, I expected that some people would respond angrily and try to close down rather than contribute to debate about the issues it raises. I also expected that they would be among the first to leap into print; and so it transpired. I had a bet with myself that someone would brandish Neville Chamberlain's umbrella, and I was not disappointed.

But I also expected the timid ones would be in the minority, and that their attempt to stifle and sideline the debate about our future in Asia would itself be sidelined. My impression is that this has happened. None of the surprisingly numerous responses to the essay, published and private, that I have seen or heard, has agreed with all that it has to say, and many have disagreed sharply with much of it. But the overwhelming majority – including those printed here – agree that Australia's situation in the Asian century is something we need to debate with an open mind and a steady eye.

I am grateful for that, but I am equally grateful for the serious, searching comments and criticisms that so many people have levelled at the essay's arguments. I would mention especially the Lowy Institute's "Interpreter" blog, which generously hosted a debate over several weeks (it can be found at http://www. lowyinterpreter.org/?d=D%20-%20Hugh%20White's%20Quarterly%20Essay). And of course I am particularly grateful to the very distinguished group who have contributed comments here, many of which go to the heart of the matter.

First, do I correctly describe the power shift? Several correspondents think I simply overstate what is going on. Let me start by agreeing unreservedly with Harry Gelber that there is nothing *inevitable* about China's economic rise. As I say in the essay, China faces many immense challenges and it is quite possible that any one of them could stop its growth. But to say that China's rise is not inevitable is after all to say very little, because policy does not deal in inevitabilities. It deals in probabilities. What matters for our debate is whether China's rise is sufficiently probable for us to take seriously its possible consequences. I argue in the essay that it is. Gelber would put the probability lower than I do. He mentions China's environmental and demographic problems, as does Lyric Hughes Hale, and I agree with them. Gelber also cites educational problems, but he needs to take another look there: China's remarkable investment in mass tertiary education is one of its most striking achievements, and one of the strongest indicators that it can keep growing beyond the first productivity step from farm to factory.

Gelber also suggests that I have overstated China's growing military power. He asks whether China could deprive the US of a serious presence in the Western Pacific, even if it wanted to. The answer is no, but it's the wrong question. If our concern is the future of US primacy in Asia, the right question is whether China can increase the costs and risks to the US of power projection into the Western Pacific to the point where these outweigh America's strategic interests here. To this question, for reasons I make clear in the essay, the answer is yes. On the other hand, America will also be able to impose high costs and risks on Chinese maritime operations. That is why I agree with Robert Kaplan that America could remain a pivotal regional power in Asia for a long time to come, while still arguing that it will lose the military capacity that has underpinned its primacy in the past.

Some people – including Geoffrey Garrett of Sydney University's United States Studies Centre writing in the *Australian* in September – have suggested that I exaggerate the power shift the other way, by overstating America's decline. Let me assure them that I do not. The essay makes quite clear that the redistribution of strategic weight in Asia is not caused by US decline. In fact, I remain quite bullish about the US. If it shows again the resilience and strength it has shown so often before, America can bounce out of its current problems and back to steady growth. But if China keeps growing for the next three decades as it has for the past three, it will still overtake America to become the largest economy in the world. That is why I say that this is not a story of American weakness, it is a story of Chinese strength.

Other commentators make a more sophisticated point. They suggest that I do not so much overstate the power shift as oversimplify it. Michael Wesley is one of them. His elegant comment reminds us that the current transformation is not simply an American or a Chinese story: Japan, India, Vietnam and others need to be brought into the picture. And he suggests that these countries will counter-balance China's growing power and make it hard for it to challenge America, and hence much less likely to try. I half agree with Michael's analysis. The half I agree with is that even if China keeps growing fast, it will not become strong enough to dominate Asia in the way that the US dominates the Western hemisphere. That is why I argued that China might be persuaded to settle for an equal share in a collective leadership rather than primacy in Asia. The half I disagree with is the conclusion Michael draws about the choices that China and America might make in future.

There are two points here. The first concerns China. Because it *cannot* dominate Asia, Michael seems to infer that it *will not* try to do so. But we cannot be sure that China will be this smart. In fact, there is a serious risk that China will get this wrong, especially because it seems so consistently to underestimate Japan as an adversary. And the risk to Asia's order does not arise only if China succeeds in dominating the region: an ultimately unsuccessful bid for primacy would be just as bad. Indeed, if it led to major war, it could be worse. So we need to work hard to persuade China not to try. That is what my "concert of power" idea aims to do.

The second point concerns America. Michael assumes I think that Asia's other players will counteract the power shift from Washington to Beijing by supporting America to constrain China's power. That is possible, but it is not to be taken for granted. The worse China behaves, the more support America will get from elsewhere in Asia. Asians will gladly support America to resist any Chinese attempt to impose a harsh Stalinist hegemony on the region. But they will be much less likely to accept the immense costs and risks of making China an adversary just to resist a Chinese bid to be treated by the US as an equal. So the support America can expect from Asians – and from Australians – will depend on whether it aims to preserve primacy or accept equality with China. In other words, the more America accepts something like my concert model of Asia's future, the more Asian support it is likely to get.

Robert Kaplan's fascinating comment – which brings to bear some of the ideas in his recent fine book *Monsoon* – starts from the same place as Wesley but heads in a different direction. He agrees that China will not be as dominant in Asia as America is in the Western hemisphere, but argues that in any competition for influence in Asia it will enjoy the decisive advantage of location. China is in Asia, which saves it the expense of projecting power into Asia across a very wide ocean. He might have added that it also makes China more willing than America to pay higher costs to achieve core objectives in Asia. The advantage of location will make China, as Kaplan says, the first among equals. But he also notes how significantly Russia could constrain China's strategic options in future. I think he is quite right, and I should have looked more closely at this question. Russia, of course, remains what Winston Churchill said it was in 1939, but my hunch is that Russia will essentially be on the defensive in its Far Eastern extremities. As long as Beijing can reassure Moscow that it has no designs on Russian territory, Moscow will do little to constrain China's ambitions in other directions.

The future dynamic of China–India relations is a different matter. On present trends India will emerge as the biggest constraint on China's power in the second half of the century, and the locus of their competition will become the strategic focus of the world. Kaplan hints in his comment, and argues in *Monsoon*, that this will be the Indian Ocean. I'm not so sure about this, and indeed find his own points about the South China Sea make a good case that it will be here rather than in the Indian Ocean that this titanic struggle will occur if it happens. Either way, nothing in Kaplan's arguments makes me any less persuaded that it is important to build an order which minimises the probability and severity of such a competition as much as possible.

Lyric Hughes Hale also suggests that we broaden the focus away from the US–China axis and look more carefully at other players. She makes the arresting and very perceptive comment that it could be Japan's rise, rather than China's, that disturbs Asia's equilibrium. She is quite right. Japan is a very big part of Asia's future, and I accept her gently implied rebuke that I should have dealt with it at greater length. After two dreadful decades Japan has still only just been overtaken by China as the world's second-largest economy, and it will remain the third-largest for decades to come. As I say in the essay, its combination of GDP and technology give it immense strategic potential, at least as an air and naval power, and of course as a nuclear power. This means that Japan is and will remain a great power in the Asian system; in other words, Asia will only be peaceful and stable if Japan is satisfied with its place in it.

There are two problems with this. First, the Japanese find it very hard to decide what would satisfy them over coming decades, and that is partly because, secondly, the outcomes that might satisfy Japan would be very uncomfortable for the rest of us. Obviously Japan would prefer to remain a strategic client of America, but Japan will not be secure, and hence will not be satisfied, as a US client if the US and China get on too well. The better those two get on, the less confident Japan can be of America's support in any clash with China, which is of course its biggest fear. These are not hypothetical questions about the distant future: they are the dilemmas posed for Japan today by incidents like the clash with China over maritime jurisdiction which has unfolded in the weeks since my essay was published. Japan caved in to Chinese pressure; how confident could it have been of US backing had it not done so?

That means the outcome the rest of us would prefer – Japan remains a US client while the US and China build a stable and trusting relationship – would not acceptable to Japan. Japan will only feel comfortable as a US client as long as it is sure it is more important to America than China is, and the bigger China becomes, the more adversarial the US–China relationship will have to be for Japan to be confident of that. In other words, Japan will only tolerate a healthy US–China relationship if it no longer relies on America for security. But the rest of us would be very nervous about Japan coming out from under America's umbrella and starting to act like a great power again for the first time since 1945. So would many in Japan itself. Hence Lyric is right that Japan's "rise" back to the status of great power could be destabilising. Apart from anything else, it could prompt America to think about withdrawing from Asia.

China's rise and Japan's strategic dependence on the US thus pose a terrible policy dilemma which would tax even the most agile and effective government.

Japan faces this dilemma at a time when its political system seems unable to deliver governments capable even of managing Japan's current international posture, let alone effecting the kinds of change needed to re-position Japan for the Asian century. Changes, when they come, are therefore likely to be abrupt and disruptive. This increases the risks to Asia's order. What can be done? I think the answer is to accept that, sixty-five years after the war, Japan is ready again to be trusted as a great power in its own right, and the rest of us – including the US and China – should gently encourage it to come back to the top table and take its place in the collective leadership of Asia that I propose. Those who do not like this idea should be prepared to offer an alternative way to satisfy Japan, or to explain how Asia can be peaceful if Japan is not satisfied.

So much for questions about the scale and nature of the power shift itself. A separate set of questions concerns the picture I paint of the order that will arise in Asia with a shift from the US to China. Gelber is one of many who think that I exaggerate the risk of intensifying contestation between the US and China, because any urge to compete will be counterbalanced by the imperatives of economic interdependence. Earlier this year I joined an extended debate on the Lowy Institute's "Interpreter" blog on this issue (www.lowyinterpreter. org/?d=D-Globalisation and war); I won't recite those arguments here. I say in the essay that interdependence does indeed *reduce* the risk of conflict by raising the cost of it, but it does not in any way *eliminate* it. To be more specific: we can rely on economic interdependence only so far as we can rely on countries to govern their conduct by rational economic self-interest. And how far is that, when questions of status and identity are involved?

In fact, I've noticed a funny thing about the interdependence argument: many people think it is decisive, but they tend to assume it applies to the other guy and not to them. Americans believe that China will still not risk the economic consequences of a strategic contest with America, while for their part the Chinese are becoming more confident that America won't in future risk the economic consequences of blocking China's path to power. Because both expect that they can achieve their strategic aims without economic sacrifice, neither sees the need to re-think these aims.

So economic self-interest is far from an infallible prophylactic against conflict between nations. Although it is a very powerful and important force for peace, it does not *remove* the need to build a new order in Asia; rather it increases the *incentive* to do so successfully. The questions of what that order would look like and how best to build it still need to be answered. If we ask ourselves what the US and China should do to best serve their mutual interest in sustained economic interdependence, the answer seems to me pretty plain. It is not to try to preserve a strategic status quo, which is increasingly out of touch with economic reality, but to build a new order which reflects their more equal economic weight – in other words, the kind of relationship of equals that I propose in the essay. The fact that this would make economic sense does not remove the big political and strategic costs that both the US and China would have to accept if it is to come about, and does not therefore remove the real risk that they will not succeed in doing it. In fact, as I argue in the essay, blind faith in interdependence as a guarantee of peace increases the risk of discord because it blinds people to the harsh reality that peace can only be guaranteed at the cost of painful compromise.

Moreover, David Uren's really interesting comment reminds us that economic imperatives can cut the other way, amplifying rather than suppressing strategic competition. This can happen in several ways, as he says: specific disputes over exchange rates and concern over access to resources can play into deeper anxieties about long-term economic "space," as Americans, and Japanese, start to worry that China will in the long term squeeze them out of manufacturing and leave them trying to sustain a high-wage economy on services alone. In other words, economics only dampens conflict as long as people remain convinced that it is a positive-sum game, and that may be less obvious in the years to come than it has been in the past.

Bruce Grant is another who believes that I am too gloomy about the risks to peace in Asia, but his argument is based on politics rather than economics. He sees the trends in Asia, and globally, leading towards a new order of multilateral cooperation through forums like the G20, rather than backwards towards the old-style power politics that I foresee. He is an optimist, in other words, and I am a pessimist. The debate between these divergent predispositions is as old as international affairs, but in today's context it can best be summarised in two questions, one analytical and the other prudential.

The analytical question is whether the kind of cooperative order that Grant and many others envisage would be more a cause or an effect of stable relations between great powers. He would argue that it is more a cause: we can be confident that the US and China will get on well because strategic contest would be incompatible with the cooperative global and regional order. I incline the other way: a cooperative order has emerged in recent decades because the great powers have got on well, and will only be preserved if they can keep doing so. If I am right, growing competition between the world's two strongest states will erode global and regional cooperation, rather than cooperation inhibiting competition. So far, sadly, the data supports my pessimism rather than Grant's optimism. Witness Copenhagen.

The prudential question is simply this: is it smarter to assume that we already have the foundations for stable US–China relations in Grant's cooperative global order, or to assume that we still need to build them? When the stakes are so high, pessimism seems more prudent, as long as it does not slip into fatalism. I do not think my pessimism does that.

Last, but by no means least, Gareth Evans' gracious and generous comment is primarily a demand for more – "a fuller, more nuanced and in some cases more persuasive discussion of the premises, precise meaning and implications" of the options for Asia's future order that I describe. How endearingly characteristic this is of the unquenchable energy and relentlessly intelligent curiosity that made Gareth such a great foreign minister. Of course he is absolutely right: there is a lot more to be said about all this – much more than even QE's indulgent editor will allow me space for here. But let me expand a little on the idea of an order based on shared leadership as the best way to secure a peaceful future for Asia.

I think many people have assumed that when I argue for Americans to relinquish primacy in Asia, I mean that they should relinquish it *to China*; that leadership in Asia would pass from America to China. In fact, I mean something very different. The collective leadership model I propose for Asia is precisely intended to *avoid* passing to China the kind of leadership that America has exercised hitherto, and at the same time to avoid a dangerous strategic contest between them. Instead we should pass it to a group which *includes* America. Membership of this group would, of course, increase China's power in Asia, but it would also constrain China's power – and offer the best prospect of doing so in a way that China might accept. It seems to me to be the only clear alternative, if China's power keeps growing, to conceding leadership to China or resisting it in a strategic contest.

Of course there are risks in this kind of cautious accommodation with China, but there are also risks in the alternatives. On one side sits passive acceptance of Chinese leadership, on the other active confrontation to deny China any increased power. We do not want to live in China's orbit; nor do we want to live in a state of hostility with China. The risks of accommodation are real, but easy to exaggerate. The risks of confrontation are, on the other hand, easy to underestimate. The risks of accommodation can be managed in an order based on shared leadership, because it provides a framework for the US to stay actively engaged, it sets clear limits to how China can use its power, and it provides clear expectations that breaches of those limits would meet a forcible response. The concert model expands China's international space, but it also imposes strong boundaries on that expanded space. And it offers a chance of doing all this peacefully.

What of human rights? I think we need to accept that working with China in a collective Asian leadership would significantly limit our capacity to press Beijing on such issues. Gareth thinks I may overstate that. Well, I hope he is right – obviously we should work hard to retain the maximum space to press China, consistent with maintaining the stable, shared regional leadership on which Asia's peace will depend. My argument is not that we should cease to press China on human rights but that we should recognise that our scope to do so – and America's scope – must take account of the need to work effectively with China *as an equal* if Asia is to remain at peace.

Which brings us back to questions of identity. In the essay I was pessimistic that Americans can bring themselves to treat China as an equal, because it is contrary to the exceptionalism which is so fundamental to America's sense of itself. I think I may have been wrong about that. In the weeks since the essay was published, I have had perhaps a dozen substantive exchanges with serious Americans from across the political spectrum who have read it. In each case – including notably the two contributions from Americans here – I have been surprised and impressed by how openly and graciously and actively they engage with its arguments and conclusions. Yet again, America's remarkable resilience – its capacity to adapt and reinvent itself – seems to be coming to the fore as it faces Asia's swift transformation. The question for Australians is whether we, who have even more at stake, can do the same.

Hugh White

Gareth Evans is chancellor of the Australian National University and a professorial fellow at the University of Melbourne. President emeritus of the International Crisis Group, he was Australia's foreign minister from 1988 to 1996.

Harry Gelber has taught international politics at Boston University, Harvard, the London School of Economics, Yale and Monash. From 1975 until 1992 he was professor of political science at the University of Tasmania. His books include *Nations out of Empires* (2001) and *Opium, Soldiers and Evangelicals* (2004).

Bruce Grant has been a foreign correspondent, columnist, academic, government adviser and diplomat. He has also written ten works of non-fiction, including *Australia's Foreign Relations* with Gareth Evans, three novels and many short stories.

Lyric Hughes Hale was founder of China Online and lives in Chicago. With her husband, David Hale, she is editor of *What's Next?*, to be published by Yale University Press in March 2011. She is a frequent visitor to Australia and a member of the Australian American Leadership Dialogue.

Robert D. Kaplan is a senior fellow at the Center for a New American Security in Washington and a national correspondent for the *Atlantic Monthly*. His most recent book is *Monsoon: The Indian Ocean and the Battle for Supremacy in the 21st Century*.

George Megalogenis is a senior writer with the *Australian* and the author of *Faultlines: Race, Work, and the Politics of Changing Australia* and *The Longest Decade*.

David Uren is the economics correspondent for the *Australian* and co-author with Lenore Taylor of *Shitstorm: Inside Labor's Darkest Days*.

Michael Wesley is the executive director of the Lowy Institute for International Policy. Previously he was professor of international relations and director of the Griffith Asia Institute. His most recent books are *Energy Security in Asia*, *The Howard Paradox: Australian Diplomacy in Asia 1996–2006* and, with Allan Gyngell, *Making Australian Foreign Policy*.

Hugh White is a professor of strategic studies at ANU and a visiting fellow at the Lowy Institute. He has been an intelligence analyst with the Office of National Assessments, a journalist with the *Sydney Morning Herald*, a senior adviser to Defence Minister Kim Beazley and Prime Minister Bob Hawke, and a senior official in the Department of Defence, where from 1995 to 2000 he was deputy secretary for strategy and intelligence and a co-author of Australia's Defence White Paper 2000.

SUBSCRIBE to Quarterly Essay & SAVE nearly 40% off the cover price

Subscriptions: Receive a discount and never miss an issue. Mailed direct to your door.

☐ **1 year subscription** (4 issues): $49 a year within Australia incl. GST. Outside Australia $79.

☐ **2 year subscription** (8 issues): $95 a year within Australia incl. GST. Outside Australia $155.

* All prices include postage and handling.

Back Issues: (Prices include postage and handling.)

☐ **QE 1** ($10.95) Robert Manne *In Denial*
☐ **QE 2** ($10.95) John Birmingham *Appeasing Jakarta*
☐ **QE 4** ($10.95) Don Watson *Rabbit Syndrome*
☐ **QE 5** ($12.95) Mungo MacCallum *Girt by Sea*
☐ **QE 6** ($12.95) John Button *Beyond Belief*
☐ **QE 7** ($12.95) John Martinkus *Paradise Betrayed*
☐ **QE 8** ($12.95) Amanda Lohrey *Groundswell*
☐ **QE 10** ($13.95) Gideon Haigh *Bad Company*
☐ **QE 11** ($13.95) Germaine Greer *Whitefella Jump Up*
☐ **QE 12** ($13.95) David Malouf *Made in England*
☐ **QE 13** ($13.95) Robert Manne with David Corlett *Sending Them Home*
☐ **QE 14** ($14.95) Paul McGeough *Mission Impossible*
☐ **QE 15** ($14.95) Margaret Simons *Latham's World*
☐ **QE 16** ($14.95) Raimond Gaita *Breach of Trust*
☐ **QE 17** ($14.95) John Hirst *"Kangaroo Court"*
☐ **QE 18** ($14.95) Gail Bell *The Worried Well*
☐ **QE 19** ($15.95) Judith Brett *Relaxed & Comfortable*
☐ **QE 20** ($15.95) John Birmingham *A Time for War*

☐ **QE 21** ($15.95) Clive Hamilton *What's Left?*
☐ **QE 22** ($15.95) Amanda Lohrey *Voting for Jesus*
☐ **QE 23** ($15.95) Inga Clendinnen *The History Question*
☐ **QE 24** ($15.95) Robyn Davidson *No Fixed Address*
☐ **QE 25** ($15.95) Peter Hartcher *Bipolar Nation*
☐ **QE 26** ($15.95) David Marr *His Master's Voice*
☐ **QE 27** ($15.95) Ian Lowe *Reaction Time*
☐ **QE 28** ($15.95) Judith Brett *Exit Right*
☐ **QE 29** ($16.95) Anne Manne *Love & Money*
☐ **QE 30** ($16.95) Paul Toohey *Last Drinks*
☐ **QE 31** ($16.95) Tim Flannery *Now or Never*
☐ **QE 32** ($16.95) Kate Jennings *American Revolution*
☐ **QE 33** ($17.95) Guy Pearse *Quarry Vision*
☐ **QE 34** ($17.95) Annabel Crabb *Stop at Nothing*
☐ **QE 35** ($17.95) Noel Pearson *Radical Hope*
☐ **QE 36** ($17.95) Mungo MacCallum *Australian Story*
☐ **QE 37** ($20.95) Waleed Aly *What's Right?*
☐ **QE 38** ($20.95) David Marr *Power Trip*
☐ **QE 39** ($20.95) Hugh White *Power Shift*

Payment Details: I enclose a cheque/money order made out to Schwartz Media Pty Ltd. Please debit my credit card (Mastercard or Visa accepted).

Card No. ☐☐☐☐ ☐☐☐☐ ☐☐☐☐ ☐☐☐☐

Expiry date   /   **Amount $**

Cardholder's name   **Signature**

Name

Address

Email   **Phone**

Post or fax this form to: Quarterly Essay, Reply Paid 79448, Melbourne VIC 3000 / Tel: (03) 9486 0288 / Fax: (03) 9486 0244 / Email: subscribe@blackincbooks.com

Subscribe online at **www.quarterlyessay.com**

www.ingramcontent.com/pod-product-compliance
Lightning Source LLC
Chambersburg PA
CBHW061237270326
41930CB00024B/3496